"In *Serving as Jesus Served*, Michele Howe app'
rary challenges. In a critical era, find timely a
as Jesus loved and make an immediate differenᴄᴇ ... ,

**—PeggySue Wells, bestselling author of 32 books,
including *The Patent* and *The Ten Best
Decisions A Single Mom Can Make***

"In Michele Howe's newest book, *Serving as Jesus Served: Practical Ways to Love Others*, she makes simple the art of service. Through real-life stories of men and women who made the choice to lay down their lives (every day), Howe guides readers into the role of a servant of Jesus Christ. Each chapter is full of inspirational stories and down-to-earth practical advice on loving those whom God has brought along your path."

**—Lucille Williams, author of *From Me to We,
The Intimacy You Crave,* and *The Impossible Kid***

"As I read *Serving as Jesus Served* by seasoned author Michele Howe, I was impressed by how we can make a difference in the lives of others by simply living our lives with the intention of being like Jesus. When we learn how to 'one-another' well by turning it into a verb, we serve as Jesus served. Michele makes this concept accessible by breaking it down into doable steps for each day and by providing examples of what it looks like lived out. This would be a great book to read with a friend to spur on life-shaping conversations."

**—Kathy Carlton Willis, God's Grin Gal,
speaker and author of multiple books, including
*Your Life on Hold: Don't Hate the Wait***

"*Serving as Jesus Served* offers new Christians and seasoned ones alike a renewed perspective on the call to serve others. Using lively stories to both inspire and challenge, Michele Howe weaves gentle, biblically based instruction throughout as she plumbs the depths of this key aspect of the Christian life."

**—Judy Roberts, writer, journalist,
and former newspaper religion editor***

SERVING AS *Jesus* SERVED

SERVING AS

SERVED

MICHELE HOWE

HENDRICKSON
PUBLISHERS

an imprint of Hendrickson Publishing Group

Serving as Jesus Served: Practical Ways to Love Others

© 2023 Michele Howe

Published by Hendrickson Publishers
an imprint of Hendrickson Publishing Group
Hendrickson Publishers, LLC
P. O. Box 3473
Peabody, Massachusetts 01961-3473
www.hendricksonpublishinggroup.com
ISBN 978-1-4964-7738-5

All rights reserved. No part of this book may be reproduced or transmitted in any form or by any means, electronic or mechanical, including photocopying, recording, or by any information storage and retrieval system, without permission in writing from the publisher.

Scripture quotations contained herein are taken from the Holy Bible, New International Version®, NIV®. Copyright © 1973, 1978, 1984, 2011 by Biblica, Inc.™ Used by permission of Zondervan. All rights reserved worldwide. www.zondervan.com. The "NIV" and "New International Version" are trademarks registered in the United States Patent and Trademark Office by Biblica, Inc.™

Photo by David Becker on Unsplash

Printed in the United States of America

First Printing — June 2023

Library of Congress Control Number: 2022948399

*Yes, L*ORD*, walking in the way of your laws, we wait for you; your name and renown are the desire of our hearts.*

Isaiah 26:8

To Jim, my husband of thirty-eight years

I want to thank you for always (and always means always) supporting me in my writing ministry. You consistently prayed for me, you made room for me to write, you are (and always have been) my go-to IT guy, and you have listened patiently to me when I sometimes wonder if I'm making any eternal difference at all. Thank you. Thank you. Thank you. I love you!

 Contents

Acknowledgments

As it is with every book I write, I am continually and with increasing measure amazed at the extraordinary giftedness that the entire Hendrickson team extends to create the book that you, dear reader, now hold in your hands. If I may, I would like to name some names so that you can be thankful right along with me for these tremendous individuals who give it their best every day, every month, year after year on every project to create a resource worthy of the Hendrickson Publishing Group's name. To start, I want to say a super-sized "Thank you!" to editorial director (and long-distance friend) Patricia Anders, who does her marvelous editorial work on my books time and time again. I both respect and admire you (and your exemplary work ethic) to produce the finest books possible.

To Dave Pietrantonio, Hendrickson's book production manager, who organizes all the behind-the-scenes production details in a seemingly effortless way, my ongoing thanks and gratitude. To Meg Rusick, Krista Squibb, and Sarah Slattery: I love that you are the same wonderfully skilled group of people who labor hard each in your individual ways to bring together a book worth far more than its selling price. That's a wondrous thing! I'm so thankful for each of you. Finally, my thanks and appreciation to my agent at the Steve Laube Agency, Bob Hostetler. You're always reminding me to dot my *i*'s and cross my *t*'s—and I thank you for that!

Lastly, no author can ever forget her dear readers. I'm humbled and grateful that the Lord has continued to allow me the privilege to write (and speak biblical truth) into people's lives about the wondrous, power-working love of Jesus. Oh, what a Savior! I have loved writing on the topic of *Serving as Jesus Served* because it has been a daily reminder of how important it is that every one of us who calls on the name of Jesus as our Lord is called to serve; that *Serving as Jesus Served* is a non-negotiable if we call ourselves Christians—and oh, what a high calling it is! To have the privilege to offer ourselves, our very lives, to him who sacrificed all to reconcile us to God the Father is a marvelous high calling indeed!

For we are God's handiwork, created in Christ Jesus to do good works, which God prepared in advance for us to do.

Ephesians 2:10

Introduction

I'm so excited to share with my family, friends, and faithful readers of many years (and many books!) my newest project, *Serving as Jesus Served: Practical Ways to Love Others.* The subject matter in this book is near and dear to my heart. As a Christian for fifty years now, I have been profoundly blessed and encouraged by faithful Christian servants who took their calling seriously and ministered to me and so many others through the years. I studied under faithful pastors who made it their life's work to diligently teach the word of God from the pulpit, thereby equipping us, the hands and feet of the church, to go out and serve others. I learned from gifted teachers in Sunday school classes and parachurch ministries how far-reaching the gospel is when each of us heeds the call to "go and make disciples," as Jesus commanded in Matthew 28.

Just as we are blessed, encouraged, and discipled by others, we likewise grow in grace and maturity when we use our gifts to serve others. Over the years, I learned invaluable life lessons as I served in the infant, toddler, and children's ministries, up until high school grades. Later, I became a small group leader of a women's Bible study group, which is still going strong some fifteen years later. The whole principle of *Serving as Jesus Served* means being on the receiving end of others' God-given gifts and talents, while we serve others using our own. This helps to build and strengthen one another so that the whole church is mature and ready to "go and make disciples" throughout the world. It's this "serve and be served" interchangeable biblical principle that makes up our local church fellowships.

I hope you'll catch the enthusiasm of reaching out to serve others wherever God has placed you today. Whether you're in the prime of life with lots of energy to extend toward others in service or you are physically weak due to age or illness, God wants to use you. Please read carefully through each of these true stories of men and women who learned to serve Jesus, no matter what challenges or obstacles they faced. God is faithful. He never calls us to a task without equipping us with everything we need to complete it. So let's get started on our journey to change our world one act of service at a time! Remember this two-part equation:

1. When we are on the receiving end of service as fellow believers obeying Jesus by using the gifts and talents given them by God, we are deeply impacted and can grow in wisdom, Bible knowledge, understanding, and application.

2. When we obey the Lord's command to serve others through his grace and strength, we in turn build up and strengthen our fellow believers so that the entire body of Christ can come to maturity.

The bottom line is this: We are called to serve—every one of us, every day. There are no exceptions to this high calling. We are saved by grace and indwelled by the Holy Spirit, who teaches us, comforts us, chastises us, and compels us to serve. What a high calling indeed!

 # Chapter 1

We Are Called to Love Others

"A new command I give you: Love one another. As I have
loved you, so you must love one another. By this everyone
will know that you are my disciples, if you love one another."
John 13:34–35

*The Lord owns every one of our relationships. He has placed
us in each one for the advancement of his kingdom and the
sake of his glory. His agenda is so much bigger and better
than ours! By his grace he is taking lost, suffering, blind,
deceived, self-absorbed, fearful, and rebellious people and
molding them into the likeness of his Son. He displays his
glory by transforming the thoughts and intentions of our
hearts. This display of glory is taking place wherever his
children—his ambassadors—live, work, and relate. Every
situation, conversation, relationship, trial, or blessing belongs
to him. We cannot be satisfied with pleasing ourselves in
what we say and do, but must ask what would please him.*

Paul David Tripp

Sara felt around the cushion edges of her recliner searching for her favorite pen—the one that seemed to disappear every time she wanted to use it. She poked and prodded the cushions until she finally spotted it. Relieved, she moved to the dining room table to get busy writing thank-you cards to the volunteers in the children's Sunday school classes.

Before she started, Sara bowed her head and prayed: *Lord, give me just the right words to bring some measure of encouragement and hope to each of my volunteers as I write today. I know them so well, and not one of them is having an easy time lately. Everyone seems to be carrying such heavy loads and many are discouraged. But Lord, they are such a faithful group of men and women. They may be weary and worn out, but they still show up early every Sunday morning to prepare and present the lessons to our children. What an eternal difference they're making! Give me the words, Lord, to let them know how much they're loved and appreciated. Amen.*

Lifting her head, Sara chose a thank-you card from her stack and began writing. She kept a current list of the volunteers and wrote some personal notes next to each person's name so that she knew what to be praying for during the week. Sara, who did not have the gift of teaching herself, deeply admired these selfless individuals who could impart the gospel and all the stories from the Old and New Testaments with flair and enthusiasm so that the children not only remembered what they were taught, but they also excitedly shared them with their families in the hallways afterward.

Sara had grown up in the church and remembered what her father had taught her about every believer being called to be a servant of the Lord. "Sara," he said, "God has given each of us a gift when we become Christians. And what do we do with gifts? We give them away! Why? To serve, to bless, and to encourage others. Never forget that God wants all of us to use the gifts he has given us so that we can help strengthen the church body one person at a time. When we don't serve, we deprive others of the gifts God wants us to use for our good and his glory." She never forgot his words—or his faithful example of service. And now, many years later, Sara was faithfully putting to use the gifts God has placed within her: the gift of encouragement, for one. Everyone who knew Sara and was on the receiving end of her uplifting thank-you cards knew it too!

Sara paints a beautiful picture of what it means to be a servant of the Lord with a calling that has eternal implications. Her understanding of the Lord's commands for all believers to be active and serving in their local fellowships is priceless. Would that every father and mother taught their own children as faithfully as Sara's did. She understood from careful study of God's word that God placed within each of his children a priceless gift—one that should be actively used to serve, bless, and encourage others.

Equally crucial to understand is that when we fail to obey God by utilizing our talents to serve others, we deprive our fellow believers by failing to enrich their lives in specific, eternally impactful ways. We weaken the local church body when we say no to service. In the real world, serving flawed people means sacrifice. It means getting our hands and feet dirty. It means learning to work with some who may not appreciate us or the way we prefer to do things. It means trusting God to equip us for his agenda, which is so much bigger and better than ours ever could be!

The bottom line is this: As Christians, service isn't an optional choice. It's simple obedience. Or for those who refuse to serve, it can mean tragic disobedience. When we serve others within our church fellowship, we're submitting to the bigger picture. We are saying yes to God's plan to be continually transformed into the image of Jesus. And as Paul Tripp concludes, "Every situation, conversation, relationship, trial, or blessing belongs to him. We cannot be satisfied with pleasing ourselves in what we say and do, but must ask what would please him." Indeed, in all things, we must continually be asking ourselves, "What would please him?"

❀ Take-away Action Thought

When I start to make excuses about why I can't or don't want to serve in my church fellowship, I will read 1 Peter 4:10–11 to remind myself that the decision not to serve is not an option. God has commanded us to serve using the gifts he has given us to bless and encourage others.

A Prayer of Confession

Dear God, thank you for choosing me to be a part of your family. I am so thankful that I am forever secure in your love and that I know I belong to you. Please help me to serve faithfully within my local church fellowship. Give me the strength, the grace, and the humility to serve wherever is needed. Help me to utilize the gifts you have given me so that I can serve, encourage, and help build up the body of Christ. I know that serving means sacrifice and that it's often exhausting. But you established the church as the family in which we use our gifts to grow into maturity and to help others grow up in grace. Be with us, Lord, as we learn how to sow seeds of service that will make an eternal impact. Amen.

Call to Action

This week, I will start each day by praying for God to give me direction and wisdom on where to serve in my local church fellowship and everywhere I journey through life. I'll then begin conversations with my church leadership about where I might be best suited to serve to bless and encourage others.

Called to Serve: We Are Called to Love Others

Monday: I'll begin my week by spending time in prayer, asking the Lord to direct me to where I should serve in my local church body.

Tuesday: I'll set up a meeting with my church leadership to discuss where I might be best suited for serving.

Wednesday: I'll review the options open to me and pray for God to show me the best place to start serving.

Thursday: I'll make a list of my closest friends and invite them over for food and fellowship with the intent of discussing how each of us can better serve at our church.

Friday: I'll read all the sections on serving that I can find in the Bible. I'll make note of the ones that stand out to me and write down the verses in my journal as a reminder that service isn't optional.

Saturday: I'll ask my friends to pray for me as I venture into new areas of service.

Sunday: On this day of reflection and rest, I'll take time to remember how many blessings I've received through the years from those who have faithfully served and through whom I was greatly blessed.

❀ Chapter 2

What Does It Look Like to Love Others?

"But seek first his kingdom and his righteousness, and all these things will be given to you as well. Therefore do not worry about tomorrow, for tomorrow will worry about itself. Each day has enough trouble of its own."

Matthew 6:33–34

A general rule about fears and anxiety is that they will not lose their power unless examined. As you do that, the more words the better. In general the more words you have for something, the more you understand it.

Edward Welch

Emily was preparing her notes to share with Mandy, her counselor in training. Having served as a biblical counselor for over twenty years, she began five years ago leading other counselors through the training courses at their church. Every Thursday afternoon, her group watched their online instruction videos and she led discussions. She guided them as they wrote their research papers and assisted them as they practiced mock counseling trials.

These training elements prepared these novice counselors to be able to work with confidence and reliance on the principles taught through God's word to address a variety of possible situations. Perhaps one of the most effective training tools Emily employed was meeting weekly with each member of her group to debrief them and spearhead any potential problems or questions they might have regarding their coursework—hence Emily's careful review and preparation now for her one-on-one meeting with Mandy.

Emily knew Mandy struggled with self-confidence in her abilities. After having met with Mandy numerous times, Emily focused on the heart of the matter—that it wasn't a lack of confidence that was the root of the issue with Mandy's hesitancy to counsel; it was fear of failure. Once Emily discovered this, she was able to counsel Mandy more effectively.

Reviewing her notes from their previous meeting, Emily read the summation of their most recent conversation: "Mandy, I've watched you counsel in our mock sessions, and you are ready to begin counseling on your own. What I believe is holding you back isn't your lack of training or experience. You're only forgetting that fear of failure is a reality for all counselors, not only new ones. Without counsel from the Spirit, we can't serve others in the most effective way. If you remember that you're just as spiritually needy on your first day of faith as you are today, then your heart and mind will be in the correct, humble posture to rely fully on God as you share these truths to others." Confident about this session with Mandy, Emily realized that she needed to hear this same truth herself.

It doesn't matter if we're new Christians or have followed Christ for many years. From the first day we accepted Jesus as Lord and Savior, we have needed his constant and steady supply of grace, strength, wisdom, and insight every hour. We always will.

Sometimes we forget that the Bible tells us that we are always in need of God's supernatural grace and strength for every task we undertake. Whether we're training for a counseling ministry such as Mandy or a veteran counselor like Emily, our inner spiritual needs are the same. Certainly, we grow, gain experience, and mature. But our inner spiritual posture should always be one of humility and complete dependence on God.

As we take on a humble and dependent posture before the Lord, we'll be able to watch our anxiety slip away. Any good we do is because God is doing the good work in and through us. Yes, we work hard to be a servant in today's world by properly training and preparing in our area of service. But as diligently as we labor, we must also be as keenly aware of our complete dependence on God to enable us to do the work set before us. We then exercise our faith by leaning fully on God's grace, knowing that it's he who equips us to complete the work.

❀ Take-away Action Thought

Today, I will begin my day by doing my best to fully prepare for the work and responsibilities before me. Part of that preparation will include spending time in prayer, asking the Lord to guide me with his wisdom, his words, and an awareness of my complete dependence on him to complete the work he has given me.

A Prayer of Confession

Dear God, I'm not sure I'll ever feel truly ready to begin serving you. I want to have the confidence and experience I need to move into this area of ministry, but I worry I'll fail. Please help me to do my part in preparing and then leave the rest in your hands. I know that although I can do all the right things to get ready, I will make mistakes. Clothe me with a humble, dependent spirit that is fully aware of how much I must rely on you every day and every hour, no matter what I put my hand to do. I am your child, and I long to honor you by trusting you because you are worthy of my trust. Amen.

Call to Action

Each morning this week, I will begin my day by reading and memorizing Matthew 6:33–34 so that when I'm tempted to worry or become afraid, it will remind me of God's command to trust him in all things and in all circumstances.

Called to Serve: What Does It Look Like to Love Others?

Monday: I'll try to recite Matthew 6:33–34 by memory and then write it down and read it when I start to worry.

Tuesday: In my journal, I'll recall past events where I wasted time and energy worrying over things that never happened. I'll also write down how God specifically met my need in supernatural ways.

Wednesday: I'll ask the Lord to reveal to me areas of troublesome anxiety. I'll confess my lack of trust and then purpose to turn from these thoughts.

Thursday: I'll contact three friends or family members and ask them how I can specifically pray for them about any areas of worry that may be troubling them.

Friday: I'll reflect on my week and ask the Lord to show me small steps of faith-building progress where I ran to him instead of wasting my time and energy worrying about imaginary troubles.

Saturday: I'll focus on studying God's word and his perfect provision and faithfulness to supply my every need. I'll recount every blessing that God has given me as I humbly and fully depend on him to equip me to serve.

Sunday: Thanksgiving and worship will be my watchwords today. I'll take time to remember the constant supply of grace, strength, wisdom, and goodness that God showered on me as I sought to serve him despite my human limitations and weaknesses.

❀ Chapter 3

We Love Others by Submitting to God's Will

> Finally, brothers and sisters, whatever is true,
> whatever is noble, whatever is right,
> whatever is pure, whatever is lovely, whatever
> is admirable—if anything is excellent
> or praiseworthy—think about such things.
>
> Philippians 4:8

> *We mistakenly look for tokens of God's love in*
> *happiness. We should instead look for*
> *them in His faithful and persistent*
> *work to conform us to Christ.*
>
> *Jerry Bridges*

When Callie and Jordan read their marriage vows to each other ten years ago, neither of them realized how difficult it would be to face the constant job relocations that the army required of Jordan. Both had dreams of living out in the countryside, in the same county they had lived their whole lives. Callie had grown up on a family farm, and she had long desired to start her married life with Jordan on one of their own. Jordan had grown up nearby, where his family owned multiple acres of farmland.

Ten years before they married, Jordan had been assured that his current post was a permanent one. Assured by the security of his past decade of service and the promise of a lasting position, Jordan asked Callie to be his wife. After long days of searching for a small hobby farm to buy, they found the right one. Delighted that God had opened the door for this homestead, Callie envisioned the many ways she would create the home of their dreams. Eighteen short months later, Jordan's superior called him into the office to tell him he was being relocated to another state to work on a special project for at least a year.

Saddened and disappointed, Jordan wondered how he would deliver the news to Callie. He didn't know how he would tell her that he didn't have a choice in the matter. Pulling into their long gravel driveway, he took a few moments to think as he gazed at the hard work Callie had done on the property, which was well on its way to feeling like home. *Lord,* he prayed, *help me to know just how to break this news to Callie. I don't want her to be devastated. Help us to trust you and your plan for us.*

After he got out his truck, he found her in the back preparing for their first delivery of baby chicks. Jordan's heart melted as he saw her. They had worked so hard to make their childhood dreams a reality, but no matter what they wished would happen, they had to leave. Somehow, he found the courage to break the news to her, and they did their best to comfort each other. Although it was difficult, they found the silver lining. And how they handled this first move became the faith foundation for all the other moves they would make in the ensuing years.

Jordan and Callie wisely made the choice to look to the Lord and trust him with their future by embracing what came that day. They understood that God's perfect plan isn't always something we can comprehend. But they did know that unless they were willing to accept the challenges and unexpected lane changes of life with trusting hearts, they wouldn't experience the vibrant faith life that Christ wanted for them. So every time Jordan was reassigned, the couple submitted their lives again and again to God's will for them. And each and every time, God blessed them and their servants' hearts in big ways.

It's true. God wants us to keep our minds on "whatever is true, whatever is noble, whatever is right, whatever is pure, whatever is lovely, whatever is admirable" (Philippians 4:8). As we serve our heavenly Father by choosing to trust him even when we don't understand, God comes close and gives us comfort, consolation, goodness, and grace to accept these unwanted, unexpected changes in life.

None of us wants to be surprised by the unexpected changes that upend us and our plans for life. But as children of the Most High, we must be willing to alter our plans, walk a new path, or even retrace our steps if that's what God is calling us to do. As servants of the Lord, we demonstrate our love for him by choosing to live any way that God deems fit. Submitting to God in service may look like moving to a new place, or it may entail staying put when we want to move. The details aren't as important as the posture of our hearts. And one of our first faith responses should be to remember that God is always working for our good (our conformity to Christ) and for his glory (so that the world might see who God is).

As Jerry Bridges says so well, "We mistakenly look for tokens of God's love in happiness. We should instead look for them in His faithful and persistent work to conform us to Christ." Our hearts can know happiness in service wherever God chooses to plant us (or uproot us), because we can be fully confident that

God only wants what is best for us and that he is the only one who knows what that best is.

 Take-away Action Thought

When God suddenly rearranges my world, I'll go directly to the Bible and spend time meditating on Philippians 4:8. I will write down anything I can think of that falls under the categories of true, noble, right, pure, lovely, admirable, excellent, and praiseworthy and then keep an ongoing list as the days go by.

A Prayer of Confession

Dear God, you call me to change my life in such drastic ways sometimes that I feel like I can't see straight. Not only do I grieve the loss of my dream, but I also feel overwhelmed by this news. Please help me to submit willingly to this life change and with full confidence that you are leading the way. I know that you only want what is the very best for me and that I am your dear child whom you love so much. Give me daily grace to accept this change and help me to keep my mind focused on all that is right and true as your word tells me to do. Thank you that I know you are always close by to give me the help I need as I seek to serve you wherever you plant me. Amen.

Call to Action

This week, I will spend time every day thinking about and writing down my thanks to God for all that is true, noble, right, pure, lovely, admirable, excellent, and praiseworthy. I will look for the good in any unexpected life changes and, by God's supernatural grace, I will find that good.

Called to Serve: We Love Others by Submitting to God's Will

Monday: I'll search out verses that bring me comfort in uncertain times, and I'll write them down to carry with me through the week.

Tuesday: I'll commit to memory one of the verses that brought me comfort in the past by reading and reciting it throughout the day until I can repeat it by memory.

Wednesday: I'll read Philippians 4:8 and thank God for each of the different categories included and then think on these blessings.

Thursday: I'll write in my journal about all the times in the past when God met me in difficult places, and then I'll reflect on his wonderful faithfulness in supplying all my needs.

Friday: I'll pray for God to prepare the way for me to serve in new ways. I'll ask him to orchestrate whatever is needed for me to be a useful servant in the coming weeks and months.

Saturday: I'll share with my family and friends the good that God is working in my heart and mind during this change. I'll encourage them in their faith walk as I tell them of God's goodness and faithfulness to me during this time of uncertainty and change.

Sunday: I'll ask the pastor and elders of my church fellowship to pray for me as I enter a new season in my life. I'll also share all of this with my church fellowship and request their prayer support as I move through these life lane changes.

 **Chapter 4**

We Love Others by Not Being Quarrelsome

Don't have anything to do with foolish and stupid arguments,
because you know they produce quarrels. And the Lord's
servant must not be quarrelsome but must be kind to
everyone, able to teach, not resentful. Opponents must be
gently instructed, in the hope that God will grant them
repentance leading them to knowledge of the truth, and
that they will come to their senses and escape from the trap
of the devil, who has taken them captive to do his will.

2 Timothy 2: 23–26

*Praise will preserve us from many evils. When the heart
is full of the praise of God, it does not have time to find
fault and grow proudly angry with others. At present
we have a great work to do and cannot come down
to bicker. Self-love and its natural irritations die in
the blaze of praise. If you praise God continually, the
vexations and troubles of life will be cheerfully borne.*

Charles Spurgeon

Diana and Craig had been married for over forty years, and as career high school teachers, they both knew how to converse with skillful persuasiveness. Diana was an English teacher as well as the debate team instructor. Craig was an upper-level mathematics teacher and baseball coach. Diana understood the power of words and how to make her point stick. Craig was into theorems and calculus principles that were logical and precise. Together, when these two educators agreed on a topic, they were unbeatable. The problem was that Diana and Craig were so confident in their own personal stances on issues that their conversations frequently deteriorated into bickering.

During their long marriage, the couple learned early on to set aside their inflexibility on those issues that were not hill-to-die-on subjects. Together they decided to adopt a kinder, gentler conversational approach with each other. It certainly required practice, but each time Diana or Craig found themselves falling back into their former unhealthy patterns, they stopped, apologized to one another, and then restarted. It worked.

Unfortunately, this lasted only until Craig's memory began to fail and he became insistent that he was always right. Diana tried to be patient, but it wasn't easy. Craig would go on and on about how he was correct about events, plans, and other family matters. Even though he was nearly always mistaken, Diana practiced listening without correcting him. She tried writing everything important on a daily wall calendar so that Craig could recall current commitments and responsibilities. But this did little to ease his growing irritability and his irrational responses to Diana when she gently attempted to remind him of conversations they already had or plans they had made.

Diana suspected that Craig was aware of his growing memory problem, and this was why he reacted so impatiently. While she understood that he was struggling, she still had to find a way to navigate through the rift between herself and her husband.

Praying daily about the problem, she realized that if Craig was slowly losing his mental abilities, then it would be left to her to keep the household in order. She needed a plan that didn't leave either of them feeling frustrated, angry, or out of sorts.

Admittedly, there were times when Diana felt like she was going crazy as she tried to listen with care and attentiveness to Craig as he rambled on. Time and again, she tried to redirect Craig's line of thinking to no avail. And when she did, they ended up arguing as they had in their first few years of marriage. Finally, during her morning time alone with God, Diana came across this passage in 2 Timothy 2: "Don't have anything to do with foolish and stupid arguments, because you know they produce quarrels. And the Lord's servant must not be quarrelsome but must be kind to everyone, able to teach, not resentful."

That was it. Diana needed to reframe how she viewed their conversations and refuse to get drawn into petty bickering and arguing any longer. It didn't do either of them any good. What she really needed was to learn to love her husband by refusing to quarrel with him even when she thought she was right and he was wrong. For that, she asked the Lord for help. From that pivotal moment, Diana was as good as her word. She did her best to refrain from getting into arguments with Craig, and it didn't take long before their former emotional closeness returned to what it once had been.

For Diana, the key to resetting their conversational pattern began with praying for the Lord to give her the grace she needed to love and serve her ailing husband, no matter how challenging it might be. She knew from being married to Craig that their marital weak point had always been communicating with gentleness, kindness, and patience. She looked back and was thankful they had changed the direction of their marriage early on by agreeing to make the effort to stop talking, start praying, and then restart communicating.

But now, the situation was different. Craig could no longer be counted on to abide by their stop, start, restart plan. Diana carried the burden of this sad shift in their relationship. So, she resolved to communicate peaceably with her husband as best she could by adopting a praise addendum to her plan. Whenever she began to feel overwhelmed by the changes in her marriage and how the two related to each other, Diana started praising God.

She did so in several different ways. She would turn on praise and worship music that reminded her of the majesty and faithfulness of God and play it in their house and car. Or she would get out her praise journal and begin jotting down each and every praiseworthy blessing she could think of—and there were always many once she got started. Finally, Diana learned to close her eyes and simply thank the Lord silently for the precious love and care he had shown them through the years.

Sometimes, though, all of her best efforts weren't enough to stop the tide of irritability and frustration that erupted from Craig. But she never gave up because she counted on the Lord to supply her with exactly what she needed moment by moment to love her husband with her words. Diana became living proof of Spurgeon's words: "If you praise God continually, the vexations and troubles of life will be cheerfully borne."

Take-away Action Thought

When I am feeling provoked to argue or fight with someone, I will call on the Lord to give me the self-control to refrain myself from falling into the downward spiral of quarreling over small matters.

A Prayer of Confession

Dear God, I am struggling so much to hold in the words I want to say to my loved one. I feel this urgency within my heart to prove that I am right. Please forgive me for not being humble enough to stop these unproductive conversations before they lead down sinful paths characterized by pride and stubbornness. Give me the self-control I need to relinquish the argument before it even begins and to accept being wrong with good grace and humility. Above all, help me to see the bigger eternal picture here. My words matter and how I use them matters. As Proverbs 18:21 states, our words are poison or fruit, and we must choose. Amen.

Call to Action

This week, I will be mindful of the words I use when conversing with others by prayerfully speaking in a way that is both humble and kind. When I feel tempted to argue a point, I will pray for God's grace to be quiet and to truly listen to what the other person is trying to communicate to me.

Called to Serve: We Love Others by Not Being Quarrelsome

Monday: I'll pray for a humble and quiet spirit to characterize all my conversations. At the end of the day, I'll reflect back on my conversations with others.

Tuesday: I'll write thank-you notes to a loved one and cite specific ways in which I've observed that person serving and loving others.

Wednesday: I'll talk to the Lord about any potential difficult conversations I may have this day. I'll ask for the wisdom to view these challenging talks from an eternal perspective.

Thursday: I'll seek peace with others, even if it means I must quiet my tongue and not make a point of correcting others' mistakes. I'll learn to "let it go" and be content that God knows what really happened.

Friday: I'll read through Proverbs, focusing on those passages that describe wise living and communicating. I'll then write down a few and carry them with me through the day.

Saturday: I'll pray for the person (or persons) with whom I have the most difficulty conversing in a calm and peaceful manner. I'll ask God to give me the wisdom and insight on how to bridge the gap that often grows between us when we disagree.

Sunday: I'll praise God through song, through my words, and through my silent prayers, giving thanks for the gift of eternal life through Jesus Christ my Savior.

 **Chapter 5**

We Love Others by Being Kind to All

Therefore, as God's chosen people, holy and dearly loved,
clothe yourselves with compassion, kindness, humility,
gentleness and patience. Bear with each other and forgive
one another if any of you has a grievance against someone.
Forgive as the Lord forgave you. And over all these virtues
put on love, which binds them all together in perfect unity.

Colossians 3:12–14

*When God's call of mercy collides with your lack of mercy, you
begin to see yourself with accuracy. You begin to confess that
you don't have inside you what God requires. You begin to
admit to yourself and others that you cannot live up to God's
standard, so you begin to cry out for the very thing that you
have refused to give to others. And as you begin to remember
that God's mercy is your only hope and you meditate on the
grandeur of the mercy that has been showered on you, you
begin to want to help others experience that same mercy.
You see, to the decree that you forget the mercy you've been
given, it is easier for you to not give mercy to others. I daily
need God's work of mercy in order to do his work of mercy.*

Paul David Tripp

*T**he apartment shouldn't be this quiet,* Jennifer thought to herself as she sorted her parents' belongings. Left box: keep. Right box: donate. With a sigh, she ventured a glance toward the spare bedroom, where she had carefully placed her parents' personal mementoes. *I don't know what's worse, Lord, the harrowing grief or the resentment. My brothers should have been here with us. Did it have to take a tragedy for them to find the time to visit? Help me, Lord. I need you to help me make it through the funeral tomorrow without losing my temper over this.*

After a few hours of distracted sorting, Jennifer felt she just couldn't do any more. With the funeral the following afternoon, she knew she needed some time alone with the Lord to read her Bible, pray, and be still. *That's enough for today. Once tomorrow is over, I can come back to finish packing everything up before the movers take away the furniture.* As she stood up, Jennifer felt weary in both body and soul. *Lord, I never imagined how alone I would feel after Mom and Dad passed.* But they were her only real family to speak of these past four years. None of her brothers ever came to visit or to help. Right now, a part of her wished she could stop them from even coming to the funeral. As the only sibling in the apartment, as it had been for the past few years, it was difficult to feel love toward any of them.

An hour later, Jennifer studied the detailed list from the funeral director and was satisfied with the arrangements. With a moment of relief, Jennifer made a cup of hot tea and sat on her sofa, staring at the fire burning before her. The dancing flames resurfaced a memory from her childhood, when they were all together, before her brothers had given up on them. *Lord, how could they go so long without seeing how they hurt us as if we meant nothing to them?* She had made every effort to tell them about Mom's dementia and Dad's instability. But everything she shared fell on deaf ears. *Help me, Lord, to let go of my resent-*

*ment for the funeral so that we can celebrate my parents' lives in
a way that will honor them and bring glory to you.*

Jennifer woke up the next morning with a clear mind and
mission. With the Lord's enabling, she was determined to walk
into the funeral home with a heart clothed in kindness toward
her brothers. She asked the Lord to imbue her with the grace
and strength to love them unconditionally. Setting aside her
personal pain, Jennifer finally experienced the blessed inner
peace that had been lacking in recent days. Hours later, she
continued to pray expectantly. God answered her prayer. Thirty
minutes before the funeral was to start, in walked her three
brothers. Jennifer looked over toward them and felt nothing
but love. Undeserved love to be sure. But something inside of
her heart had dramatically shifted. When she saw her brothers'
faces, she knew she still had family in this world, and they were
worth fighting for, even though they had failed to love and serve
their parents. Tentatively eyeing their sister and waiting for her
reaction, they must have seen something akin to tenderness in
her eyes, because they moved toward her and the four embraced
for a long time before letting go.

Being a true servant of the Lord means offering kindness
and mercy to those who don't deserve it. This rare expression
of unconditional love accompanied by full and free forgiveness
is not a take-it or leave-it option for those in Christ. Is it easy?
Is it offered without cost to oneself? No and no. And yet God
commands us to be kind and merciful and to forgive others.

As Jennifer worked through her own emotions of disappointment and resentment toward her brothers over their lack of
service toward their parents, she discovered the truth that set

her free from the inside. Jennifer recognized that because she was fully forgiven by God and offered mercy upon mercy every day of her life, she was compelled to do the same for the sake of Christ. Is it possible to truly forgive and then forget the painful offenses of others who have caused us great personal pain? It is indeed possible for those who have been forgiven themselves.

Jennifer asked the Lord to enable her to fully forgive, and the moment arrived when she had to face her wayward brothers. She knew God was answering her heartfelt plea. She was able to see past her brothers' failings and the immense pain it had caused so that she could truly see them in a new light. Jennifer, by the grace of God, opened the door to their familial relationship. As she did, she learned much about each of her siblings and the guilt and sorrow they felt over their lack of commitment to their parents. Jennifer hadn't needed to shower them with more condemnation because God was already convicting their hearts. Instead, through her love shown in kindness and mercy, Jennifer was able to open the lines of communication about her own struggles, her own failings, and then share her faith in Christ. To this day, she remembers how God enabled her to demonstrate Christlike mercy and forgiveness to her brothers, which eventually was pivotal in them coming to their own relationship with Jesus Christ.

As Jennifer later reflected on this emotionally intense time, she never stopped giving thanks for God's orchestration of events, his abiding presence, and his merciful answer to her prayer for supernatural grace to demonstrate unconditional love laced with kindness and mercy toward her brothers. That day, God's grace changed everything. It always does.

 Take-away Action Thought

When I'm confronted with disappointment over others' failings, I'll reflect on the mercy that God has shown me and continues to lavish on me. My personal admission of my own failings will give me the perspective I need to forgive others, fully and freely, of their transgressions.

A Prayer of Confession

Dear God, I cannot hide from you the feelings that I am experiencing when I think about my family's failure to serve one another. I'm upset that I feel alone in my love for them. Please give me the grace I need to forgive them because I am forgiven fully and freely by you. When I reflect on your mercy toward me, I can't refuse to offer that same merciful forgiveness toward others. Let goodness and mercy follow me all the days of my life, and may I extend these precious gifts to everyone. Amen.

Call to Action

Kindness and mercy will go hand in hand this week as I seek to love, serve, and forgive those with whom I interact at home, at work, and wherever my feet may step.

Called to Serve: We Love Others by Being Kind to All

Monday: I'll begin my week with a day of prayerful confession to God about anyone with whom I've harbored anger or resentment, and then I'll pray for this person to know God's saving love in a personal way.

Tuesday: I'll be proactive with my words by speaking kindly to all, even when provoked.

Wednesday: I'll demonstrate kindness through an act of service for someone in my home and in my workplace.

Thursday: I'll search through my closet and find good clothing items to give away to a local shelter.

Friday: I'll invite someone over for coffee and/or a meal.

Saturday: I'll go through my contact list and reach out to a family member or friend with whom I've lost touch to find out how they're doing.

Sunday: During my fellowship service at church, I'll be sure to offer encouragement through a kind word to my pastor and everyone who serves on staff.

 **Chapter 6**

We Love Others by Encouraging
Them to Trust God

Rejoice in the Lord always. I will say it again: Rejoice! Let
your gentleness be evident to all. The Lord is near. Do not
be anxious about anything, but in every situation, by prayer
and petition, with thanksgiving, present your requests to God.
And the peace of God, which transcends all understanding,
will guard your hearts and your minds in Christ Jesus.

Philippians 4:4–7

God lives in perfect calm and contentment. Why?
Because He's in charge of everything and can operate
everything perfectly according to His will. Since He is
omniscient, He is never surprised. Nothing can threaten
His omnipotence. No possible sin can stain His holiness.
Even His wrath is clear, controlled, and confident. There
is no regret in His mind; for He has never done, said, or
thought anything that He would change in any way.

John MacArthur

Some years ago, when my husband and I were entering the "empty nest" season of life, I wrote a book titled *Empty Nest, What's Next? Parenting Adult Children without Losing Your Mind.* In this book, one of the principles I discuss is helping dads and moms learn how to transition from being frontline parents to sideline parents. Meaning what? In short, once our children reach adulthood, it's time to move ourselves from the front and center of their lives (in every aspect of their lives) to the sidelines (where we are still involved, observing, and ready to assist but in a more intentionally removed way).

Well, clearly this principle doesn't get simpler over time. In the last week alone, two of my children (both now in their thirties) kindly reminded me that I don't need to be "Mom Fix-It" anymore. What they both expressed to me was that they want me to listen and love and care, but to resist trying to fix-it, whatever "it" might be. Oh, the trials of motherhood! What mother doesn't want to jump in with both hands and feet and go where wiser individuals know better than to tread?

For me, watching my adult children go through trials and suffering cuts me to the core. It doesn't matter that I know that God always uses whatever hardships he allows to continue the ongoing process of sanctification. I know this to be true because the Bible is full of real accounts and numerous promises that state this very principle. My struggle comes when I know that God wants me to take my hands off a problem and to trust him, and then encourage my children to trust him too.

As my daughters explained to me (on two separate occasions), they just need a listening ear—not a plan of action meticulously formulated. So what's a mom to do? Well, I'm going back to basics. Once again, I'm asking the Lord to help me move to the sidelines of my adult children's lives, unless they come to me seeking counsel and advice. I will take my concerns, their burdens (which become my burdens by default when I don't trust the Lord) and their trials directly to the Lord—and leave them there. As my loving husband often reminds me, the things our children go through are fantastic opportunities for the Lord to work deeply and effectively in their lives—for their good and his glory. So be encouraged! As John MacArthur says, "God is in charge of everything and can operate everything perfectly according to His will."

I realize that intentionally moving ourselves from the frontline to the sidelines of our loved ones' lives is much more difficult than simply deciding to do so. However, even amid deep emotional pain, mental stress, and spiritual battle, it is important that we remember another sound biblical principle: circles. Yes, circles. We each have a small circle of responsibility that generally includes our families and our close friends. But we have a second circle too. We call it the circle of care. This circle is much larger and encompasses not only our immediate family and close friends but also extends out much farther afield.

For example, on a day-to-day basis, I care for my spouse, my children, and grandchildren, my immediate family, and close friends. But I also desire to serve and care for others whom God has placed in my life, such as my neighbors, work colleagues, fellow students, church members, and so on. This second circle is one that I have to view differently from my small circle of responsibility. My larger circle of care means that I'm not the one responsible to make all the hurt and pain and suffering go away. I may not even be the one who can lift their burdens in any practical way. I can, however, pray and take my petitions directly to the Lord, who lives to intercede on their behalf.

The beauty of understanding this circle distinction is that I realize it's not up to me to be Mom Fix-It or Friend Fix-It or even Neighbor Fix-It. Only God can "fix" the deepest levels of our souls through the saving work that Jesus accomplished on the cross. Only God is omnipotent and omnipresent and wields the power to change people's lives. The sooner I accept this comforting truth, the better.

It's also better for my children and all the other folks I care about, where too often I try to put my oar in where it doesn't belong. I've always remembered a quotation I heard many years ago. The gist of it is this: sometimes God doesn't want us muddying the waters by jumping in to fix other people's problems, because he placed them there for their ultimate good. When I jump in to help, my dear children or friends may not gain the wisdom, insight, and experience that God intended. Knowing this gives me the wisdom to listen, love, and care, which leads me then to encourage them to trust God.

❀ Take-away Action Thought

When I'm tempted to jump in and try to fix things, I will stop and pray instead. I will remind myself that God is omnipotent and omnipresent and that he is taking care of those I love.

A Prayer of Confession

Dear God, I'm so tempted to try to make everything all right for my loved ones. I want to make all their pain and suffering disappear. But I know that you never waste an ounce of pain that we endure. You always use whatever challenges and difficulties we face for our good and your glory. I know this to be true. Your word declares this time and time again, which is why I choose to trust you even when my heart is breaking over something my dear one is facing. Give me your divine wisdom and faith to put all my trust in you and your plans. Help me to leave my burdens at your feet and encourage those I love to trust you too. Amen.

Call to Action

When I feel tempted to run toward a situation to fix it, I will remember that only God can bring healing and health and well-being to a person. I will pray before I enter a situation and ask God to show me how I can best encourage my dear one to put the full weight of their trust in him, even before they seek release from its painful grip.

Called to Serve: We Love Others by Encouraging Them to Trust God

Monday: I'll start my day by writing in my journal and prayer-fully making note of everyone on my heart. I'll then pray for God to intervene as he sees fit and trust that his way is always perfect.

Tuesday: I'll review my prayer list of people and separate them into the two circles—the circle of responsibility and the circle of care. I'll then make sure I'm conscious of the distinction between the two and how I interact with each one.

Wednesday: Referring to my circle of responsibility, I'll pray about how I can bring encouragement and hope to my dear ones and then make practical plans to do so.

Thursday: Referring to my circle of care, I'll pray for each person I've included and write a note of encouragement to them.

Friday: I'll look up verses that describe God's omnipotence and omnipresence and study them as an encouragement to trust my all-powerful, ever-present heavenly Father.

Saturday: I'll find several verses on encouragement and on trusting God in all circumstances and then write a short note to those in my circle of responsibility and care.

Sunday: I'll reflect on the previous week and how I witnessed God at work in my life and in the lives of those I love. I'll then write down these blessings in my journal and give thanks.

 **Chapter 7**

We Love Others by Being Patient When Wronged

Then [Jesus] said to them all: "Whoever wants to be my
disciple must deny themselves and take up their cross
daily and follow me. For whoever wants to save their life
will lose it, but whoever loses their life for me will save it."

Luke 9:23–24

*Taking up crosses daily doesn't mean making one
big once-and-for-all sacrifice and get it over with. It
means repeatedly, over and over again, day after
day and year after year, saying no to present desires
and plans in order to say yes to God and others.*

Randy Alcorn

Dean woke up on Father's Day morning grateful that God
had answered his prayers to bring his stepson, Kyle,
back into his life. After the death of his wife, Annie two
years prior, Dean had tried to connect with Kyle. Having raised
him from the time he was five-years-old, Dean was the only
father his stepson had known.

Dean and Annie met at church when Kyle was just turning five, and it didn't take long for them to create a family. For Dean, it was idyllic. He loved Annie, and he loved Kyle as if he were his own son. Dean became Kyle's Boys Brigade leader, and he took him fishing in the summer and snow skiing in the winter. They did everything together. In fact, the two even looked alike! His relationships with Annie and his stepson made Dean one happy and fulfilled man.

All had been well until Annie began developing serious heart problems, which escalated over the years. After numerous operations to correct her failing heart, Annie and Dean finally faced the fact that unless God intervened, she wouldn't live to see Kyle grow to manhood. By this time, Kyle was a teenager. As he observed his mom grow weaker and sicker by the month, Kyle began to distance himself from both Dean and Annie. It was heartbreaking for his parents, who tried in vain to repair the relationship, although Kyle had emotionally closed himself off from them. Nothing they did broke through his increasingly cold, angry demeanor.

A week before Kyle's eighteenth birthday, Annie passed away in her sleep. Rousing Kyle and delivering the news was the hardest task Dean had ever undertaken. Kyle stormed from the house and was absent for three days, nearly missing his mother's funeral. On the day of the service, Dean tried again to reach into Kyle's grieving heart by assuring him of his love, but Kyle didn't say much and was gone in the morning.

Dean did everything possible to locate his missing son in the months that followed. Finally, after every search was exhausted, police told Dean that there was nothing more they could do. He tried to rebuild his shattered life without his wife or his son by his side. Day after day, Dean cried out to the Lord and begged him to bring Kyle home. Although the authorities gave up looking for Kyle, Dean didn't. His father's heart wouldn't stop searching for his wayward son.

Some twenty months later, without any prior warning or announcement, Kyle came home. When Dean opened the front door, he was shocked to see Kyle standing there, but he pulled him in close and held him for a long time. That evening, they wept and talked late into the night. Repentant and sorrowful for his reckless behavior, Kyle asked for Dean's forgiveness. All of this took place the night before Father's Day—the day Dean had been dreading. Instead, God had mercifully answered this hurting father's prayer and what a day of rejoicing it was!

On Father's Day, Kyle and Dean grilled steaks with all the sides and later consumed a quart of ice cream. Having observed how thin Kyle had become, Dean was determined to put some weight back on his once-athletic son. They made plans together for getting Kyle into an electrician's apprentice program he had talked about while in high school. They even planned to take a trip to the mountains to camp and fish before the summer was out.

But the most important conversation on those first days together was trying to understand why Kyle felt compelled to run away after his mom died. Dean carefully listened and wisely said little as he tried to comprehend Kyle's reasons. Dean's thoughts fluctuated between heartfelt gratitude that Kyle was home and "What were you thinking?"

For months, Dean had privately reflected on how he would react if Kyle returned home. Thankfully, he had responded with kindness and compassion. But now, as the shock of Kyle's homecoming was starting to fade, Dean realized he had to keep a check on the attitude of his heart by not allowing any bitterness or resentment to settle in. So he prayed, *Lord, thank you for bringing my son home to me. Please help me to love him well and to continue to invest in our relationship as I've always done. Don't allow any anger or bitterness to take root in my heart. My life is yours; it always has been. Let me live it for your glory one day at a time. Amen.* Dean lived up to this prayer—one day at a time.

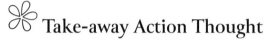 ## Take-away Action Thought

When I start to feel anger or resentment take root in my heart, I will remind myself that my life belongs to Jesus, and I will offer it up one day at a time come what may. I will be purposeful about losing my life in order to gain it.

A Pray of Confession

Dear God, today was a mix of intense emotions. I felt such joy and gratitude at the reconciliation of my loved one. Thank you! But I'm also feeling some residual anger over the pain this person put me through by their sinful choices. Help me to take captive every thought and to forgive this person many times over. Help me to lay down my life every day for the sake of others. And please help me to guard my heart one thought at a time so that no root of bitterness will ever take root and grow. Amen.

Call to Action

Each day this week, I'll begin by praying for the grace and strength to lay down my life for Christ. I will ask the Lord to give me the strength to serve selflessly and to be patient even when wronged.

Called to Serve: We Love Others by Being Patient When Wronged

Monday: This week, I'll focus on examining my heart and mind to see if I'm holding any resentment against those who have hurt me. I'll ask the Lord to reveal this sin to my heart and confess as needed.

Tuesday: I'll start a word study in Scripture on the dangers of allowing bitterness and resentment against others to flourish in my heart and how these sins spread and subsequently defile many.

Wednesday: I'll start my day by asking the Lord to help me be especially mindful about picking up my cross daily so that I seek to serve others rather than myself.

Thursday: I'll spend time with God in prayer, asking him to bring to my mind anyone with whom I've had a disagreement, and then I'll pray for that person's needs.

Friday: I'll consider the family and friends in my life with whom I struggle to exhibit patience. I'll find new ways to demonstrate my love and care for each of them in practical ways.

Saturday: As I reflect on my week, I'll go over my personal interactions with others and make amends and seek forgiveness if I failed to love unconditionally or with a patient attitude.

Sunday: I'll get out my journal and spend time recalling and then meditating on the countless ways Jesus took up his cross by preferring the needs of others before his own.

 # Chapter 8

We Love Others by Enduring Hardship

As servants of God we commend ourselves in every
way: in great endurance; in troubles, hardships and
distresses; in beatings, imprisonments and riots; in
hard work, sleepless nights and hunger; in purity,
understanding, patience and kindness; in the Holy Spirit
and in sincere love; in truthful speech and in the power
of God; with weapons of righteousness in the right hand
and in the left . . . sorrowful, yet always rejoicing.

2 Corinthians 6:4–7, 10

*Unfortunately, we are comfortable not being in the know.
We do not like living by faith. We want to know outcomes
before we begin. We want to know it will be okay before
we move forward. We want to work within our abilities
rather than the Lord's strength. We are no different from
the disciples. God is calling you to trust Him—to walk
by faith. He will not give you all the answers you desire.
If He did, you would be back to trusting yourself again.
He is calling you to stop trusting yourself. Nothing will
bring clarity to this faith tension like the gospel story.*

Rick Thomas

Meg busied herself in the kitchen after dinner, still fuming after the latest conversation she had with her adult daughter, Kelsey. *Why Lord? Why does every single conversation with her end in tears or anger? I know how frustrating it can be as a single woman wanting a family, but she doesn't acknowledge the good in her life that you have given her.* Meg took a last glance around the kitchen and then went into her library to finish up the paperwork she had begun earlier.

Rifling through the volunteer application forms for their church's in house daycare ministry, Meg felt grateful for the women who had stepped up to work one half day a week caring for the children of their fellowship's single mothers. As a not-for-profit ministry to these single moms, Meg marveled at the faithfulness of God who always provided the volunteer staff they needed so that these single mothers were able to drop off their precious little ones, confident they would be well cared for by fellow believers.

As Meg studied the applications, she couldn't stop her mind from drifting back to Kelsey. *How is it that I can run this ministry, but never communicate well with my own daughter? How long can our relationship take this constant tension? Lord, help me to show my love for her. I have been dreading these conversations with her for far too long. Give me your wisdom. Give me your grace, please.*

Setting aside the forms for a minute, Meg took a deep breath and decided that what she needed most was a good word from the Lord. So she grabbed her Bible and retreated to her favorite comfy recliner near the window and opened her Bible to the book of Psalms. Reading through five psalms a day had been her habit for many years, and she knew that as she lingered in each psalm and allowed its soothing truth to permeate her troubled heart and mind, she would calm down and see this troubling situation in a fresh light.

As Meg pondered the great truths that God is always close by and actively listening to her cries for help, she found herself exhaling much of the internal tension she had been holding inside. Praying for Kelsey came so much easier when Meg was able to focus on God's faithfulness. *Lord, please help me to never lose hope that Kelsey will grow in maturity and faith. I want so much more for her than what she is experiencing right now in her life. She needs you to be her focus and center. But the longer this goes on, the more bitter she will become about what she thinks is missing in her life. Give me your wisdom, your words, and your gracious Spirit to help guide me every time I speak with her. Let my words serve you, Jesus, by pointing her directly to you. Amen.*

Sometimes observing the difficulties of those we love can affect us more deeply than our own trials. As Meg discovered, Kelsey's struggles affected her in similar measure because Meg felt helpless to change the way Kelsey perceived her disappointment at being single. Meg longed for her daughter to experience a significant breakthrough in her life. She prayed diligently every day for God to do a work in her daughter's heart and mind. But even today, all of Meg's hopes and dreams for her child were just that: hopes and dreams.

Still, Meg was learning an important lesson through all of her difficult and tense conversations with Kelsey. She was beginning to understand that the internal battle that Kelsey fought each day to trust God was not unlike her own battle of the mind. As Kelsey's mother, Meg empathized with her adult child's struggles to maintain sound biblical thinking despite daily troubles. She also fought a daily battle against discouragement and hopelessness. Kelsey was discontent because she was still single, and Meg was discontent because she wanted Kelsey to be happy. Neither one was trusting God or his divine purposes.

Like many of us, when we experience one disappointment after another, it's challenging to continue to trust God and express a grateful heart day after day. Life is hard, and disappointments are more the rule than the exception. And yet, as we turn toward the Lord in our sorrow and on behalf of others, God's promises of perfect provision shine brightly against the backdrop of pain and suffering. As 2 Corinthians 6:10 states, we can live, "sorrowful, yet always rejoicing." We can rise to this blessed place of contentment and peace even in the midst of hopeless situations that don't appear to have any definite resolution or end date. Meg came to the place where she understood that the best way to serve her daughter was to keep reminding her of who Jesus is and who he promised to be for her. So she did. Meg made it her primary mission to speak life into her daughter's heart every time they talked. And she prayed, too, for God to reveal to Kelsey his heart of love so that she would also learn to trust him.

❀ Take-away Action Thought

When I'm experiencing hardship, I will discipline my heart and mind to find my rest, my peace, and my contentment through the daily study of God's word and retreat to the book of Psalms for comfort and assurance.

A Prayer of Confession

Dear God, I must ask for your forgiveness for trying to remedy whatever I believe is broken or missing in my loved one's life. I want to rush in and make reparations and take all their pain away. In truth, I want them to be happy. But, Lord, I know better. I must trust you above all that I can see with my eyes. Help me to learn that I can best serve you today by speaking words of truth and faith-driven encouragement to my beloved one. They need to turn to you for their comfort and strength as they face difficulties and disappointments. Give me your words of life to impart to them and never let me forget that you are close by and attentive to my every prayer. Amen.

Call to Action

In the midst of circumstances that are characterized by hardship, I will be intentional about speaking words of life and truth to everyone with whom I interact.

Called to Serve: We Love Others by Enduring Hardship

Monday: I won't allow thoughts of complaint or discontent to take root in my heart or mind.

Tuesday: I'll turn the tables on my difficulties by giving thanks for each one and by asking the Lord to show me what he may be doing in me by allowing these hardships.

Wednesday: When I speak to others, I'll be mindful to tell them about God's enduring love and daily faithfulness to me and share those blessings with them.

Thursday: I'll spend time praying for my family and friends, asking God to show himself strong on their behalf in the midst of their pain and suffering.

Friday: I'll write several notes of encouragement to those I know are going through hard times, and I'll include a specific verse of Scripture that declares God's promise of perfect provision.

Saturday: If there are practical ways in which I can ease another's burden, I'll make plans to do so.

Sunday: During my fellowship time at church, I'll seek out anyone I know going through a rough time and offer to pray with and for them.

 **Chapter 9**

We Love Others by Laboring Selflessly

You, my brothers and sisters, were called to be free. But do
not use your freedom to indulge the flesh; rather, serve one
another humbly in love. For the entire law is fulfilled in
keeping this one command: "Love your neighbor as yourself."

Galatians 5:13–14

*The Bible really is a story of kingdoms in conflict, and that
battle rages on the field of your heart. One kingdom leads
you to the King of kings and the others sets you up as king.
The big kingdom works to dethrone you and decimate your
little kingdom of one, while the little kingdom seduces you
with promises it cannot deliver. You either pray that God's
kingdom will come and that his will be done or you work
to make sure that your will and your way win the day.*

Paul David Tripp

Janna was deep asleep when she felt a persistent tug on her
arm. "Grandma! Grandma! Wake up! I had a nightmare,"
five-year-old Nora whispered. Taking her granddaughter
into her arms, Janna comforted little Nora until she settled down,
and then walked her back downstairs to her own room. Quietly

making her way back to her own attached apartment, Janna returned to her bed, but sleep evaded her. For several hours, Janna tossed and turned and was unable to drift back to sleep until the early morning hours.

Just when Janna felt relaxed enough to sleep, she heard the patter of footsteps coming up her stairs and groaned. *I'm so tired*, she thought, *and what a day I have ahead of me.* Rousing herself and grabbing her bathrobe, Janna was greeted by both of her grandchildren, who were already chattering about what they had planned for the morning ahead. Janna smiled wanly and down the stairs they trekked together for breakfast.

As Janna sat with her daughter and their family during breakfast, she sipped her coffee appreciatively. *There was so much to do*, she thought. *It feels like one interruption after another, and I can't ever catch up. I love my grandchildren dearly, but sometimes I wonder if I have the energy to keep pace with their lives and my own.*

Sighing, Janna got up and cleaned away the dishes before returning to her apartment to prepare for the day. Alone again, Janna's glance landed on her desk piled ever higher with her to-do tasks. Again, she sighed. But this time it was a happy, thankful breath of release. Janna couldn't help but notice her burgeoning list of incomplete responsibilities, but what caught and kept her attention was two photos of her grandchildren's faces smiling back at her. *Yes, Lord, I hear you. Message received.* Her grandkids may zap her energy, but they are worth far more than any amount of satisfaction she finds when she's completed her daily to-do list.

Janna struggled with this daily annoyance more than she first realized. After her daughter and son-in-law invited her to move in, Janna had to reckon with more than interruptions and unfinished work projects. She soon came to realize that it was her heart that needed a talking to. Her grandchildren ran to Grandma Janna when they needed help, a listening ear, or a warm embrace. And Janna loved this intimate up-close-and-personal grandparenting role.

However, like all of us, Janna also realized that her own responsibilities often got neglected during the course of the day. So Janna, like us, had to choose. Would she choose to set aside the non-essential tasks that she hoped to accomplish in favor of serving her family? Would she sometimes set aside her to-do lists so that she could invest in the living blessings that need her time and attention?

It doesn't matter if we're single, married, with children or without. God wants us to be willing to set aside our preferences for how we spend our hours and our days when people (of the little or big variety) come to us for help, for love, for a good word. We need to be willing to say "Thy will be done" every single day. Schedules will be interrupted. Sleep will be lost. Material goods might be broken. Our to-do list might grow longer than we hoped. But we will never regret placing people before projects.

So today, let each of us ask God for the wisdom and the grace to set aside our cherished plans as the needs arise. Let us ask him for the strength to selflessly labor hard on behalf of those he has brought close to us. And as we choose to invest in our people above our projects, we will see God blessing our efforts and multiplying them into eternity.

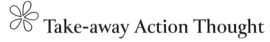 Take-away Action Thought

When I feel frustrated because I can't get everything done that I had planned on accomplishing, I will begin giving thanks for the blessing and privilege of investing in people over projects.

A Prayer of Confession

Dear God, please help me to see what is truly most important in my life. Help me to always choose to relinquish my own desires in favor of loving and serving those precious people you have placed in my life. Give me an eager willingness to set aside my cherished plans so that I can be up close and personal in loving my family and friends. Make my heart willing to submit to your will each and every day. I love you, Lord, and I want to share your bounteous love with those I love. May my investment always be that of the eternal sort.

Call to Action

At the beginning of this day, I will prayerfully review my commitments and choose to place people over my projects as much as I am able.

Called to Serve: We Love Others by Laboring Selflessly

Monday: I'll prayerfully review the upcoming week and make needed adjustments so that I have time every day to love and serve my family.

Tuesday: I'll make time at some point today for rest, recreation, and play with my dear ones.

Wednesday: I'll make a list of my loved ones and write down their specific prayer needs, and I'll pray for them before bed.

Thursday: I'll pray that I can happily submit to God's will for me on this day, even if I have to rearrange my schedule or set aside my tasks because I'm needed elsewhere.

Friday: I'll reflect back on my week, taking note of my heart attitude and any moments when I became frustrated by interruptions or had to stop what I was doing. I'll confess these heart issues and pray for God's grace and wisdom to handle these inevitable interruptions better the next time.

Saturday: I'll talk with my loved ones about their week and then ask to sit and pray with them.

Sunday: I will rest. As much as I can, I'll spend today contemplating God's goodness and nurture a quiet, calm, and peaceful spirit.

✿ Chapter 10

We Love Others by Waiting Well

Be patient, then, brothers and sisters, until the
Lord's coming. See how the farmer waits for the land
to yield its valuable crop, patiently waiting for the
autumn and spring rains. You too, be patient and
stand firm, because the Lord's coming is near.

James 5:7–8

*God is God. God is a three-personed God. He loves us. We are
not adrift in chaos. To me that is the most fortifying, the most
stabilizing, the most peace-giving thing that I know anything
about in the universe. Every time things have seemingly
fallen apart in my life, I have gone back to those things that
do not change. Nothing in the universe can ever change
those facts. He loves me. I am not at the mercy of chance.*

Elisabeth Elliot

These days, it seems as though everyone is waiting for
something. We're waiting for loved ones to come to saving
faith in Christ. We're waiting for those we love to chart
a different course in their lives because the path they're on is
destructive. We're waiting for God to answer our prayers. We're

waiting for God to rescue us from circumstances that are so overwhelming that we struggle to sleep at night. From the large to the small, we're waiting for relief and help and renewed hope.

The universal question to our waiting is this: Are we waiting well? To be more precise, what does it mean to wait well? I believe that waiting well means trusting in the Triune God who loves us and who hasn't set us adrift in chaos. As Elisabeth Elliot so eloquently wrote, "God is God. . . . To me that is the most fortifying, the most stabilizing, the most peace-giving thing that I know anything about in the universe." I agree. To know that the God I love and serve loves me, and that I am not cast adrift to face the worst life has to offer fortifies me, stabilizes me, and gives me peace so that I can lay my head down every night and rest in his perfect provision.

As life-giving and powerful as this truth is to me, however, I still fight a daily battle with anxiety. And to boot, I hate waiting! Why? How can I doubt his care for me when God sent his only Son to die a horrific death in my place? The answer is simple: I continue to hold onto the illusion that I have control of my life. I wrestle with the biblical truth that only God is in complete control. And while this truth comforts me, I also know that God desires my highest good, which means that the suffering and trials that come will conform me into the image of his dear Son Jesus. This can feel a little scary. The suffering and trials part, that is.

So each morning, I start my day by giving thanks to God for his presence in my life. I tell him how grateful I am that he is ruler over all. I confess to the areas where I'm still vying for control over my life. I ask him for the grace, wisdom, and strength to relinquish my cherished plans and deeply held desires in favor of his perfect plan for me that day. I then ask for the grace to wait well and to never cease praying for those he has placed on my heart and mind.

Serving others means learning what it means to wait well. No matter what we're waiting for (the salvation of loved ones or relief from pain and suffering in all its many varieties), the posture of our hearts matters. We can only wait well and in complete trust in God when we're sure of his righteousness, goodness, and perfect love for us. How can we know and trust in God's character when life seems out of control? By opening our Bible and reading it; we pour over the Scripture verses that tell of God's righteousness, goodness, and his perfect love for us.

I can't count the number of conversations I've had with fellow believers who are in a pit of despair but who admit that they rarely open their Bible to get to know their heavenly Father. It's impossible to trust someone we don't really know. It doesn't even make sense to say we are Christians who love Jesus if we fail to obey one his most basic commands: that of renewing our minds daily by searching Scripture and meditating on its powerful truths. We need to remember this: We have to invest time and energy in knowing who God is by consistently spending time in his word so that we can rightly interpret life and all of its circumstances. We learn to wait well when we learn to reframe our pain from an eternal lens.

We must ask ourselves if we're growing into those types of Christians who have learned to wait well despite what their physical eyes see all around them. As Jesus told his disciple Thomas when he doubted, "Because you have seen me, you have believed; blessed are those who have not seen and yet have believed" (John 20:29). Yes, we too can believe even if we haven't seen. And through the gracious empowering of the Holy Spirit, we can live in confidence of God's faithfulness and perfect provision even before we see the answers to our prayers on this physical plain. As James writes, "Be patient and stand firm, because the Lord's coming is near."

 Take-away Action Thought

When I start to waver in unbelief and doubt, I will go to the Bible to find my refuge and strength as I pour over the accounts of God's faithfulness and perfect love. I'll linger in these amazing passages and let the powerful truth of who God is reach deeply into my hurting heart and soul.

A Prayer of Confession

Dear God, please help me to be constant in my faith as I learn how to wait well. I have been coming to you for so long for my greatest troubles, and I do believe that you hear my every prayer. But sometimes I wonder how much longer I'll have to wait before you answer my prayer. Give me the wisdom and understanding I need to rest fully on your trustworthy character and to spend time every day pouring over your precious words of life. I'm adrift without your Spirit's guidance to help me to reframe the hardships I face every day. I love you. I trust you. Help me to learn to wait well and honor you as I do. Amen.

Call to Action

Every evening this week, before I go to sleep, I'll read a story from Scripture that tells of God's supernatural work in the lives of his faithful followers. I'll meditate on how God worked above and beyond his children's expectations to accomplish his perfect will for them.

Called to Serve: We Love Others by Waiting Well

Monday: I'll begin my week by remembering one specific event where God showed his faithfulness and perfect love toward me in what I considered a difficult and frightening situation.

Tuesday: I'll read a story from both the Old Testament and the New Testament that describes how God worked in miraculous ways to love and protect his people.

Wednesday: In my journal, I'll express any unanswered prayers, and write out verses on prayer to help me fight against doubt or discouragement.

Thursday: I'll reflect on God's character by reading verses that describe him expansively and magnificently.

Friday: I'll confess to the Lord those times when I've been impatient or doubted his perfect love for me. I'll then ask Jesus to give me a renewed hunger for his words of life.

Saturday: I'll choose one verse that speaks of God's majesty and memorize it. I'll then write it on a card to carry with me throughout the day.

Sunday: I'll give thanks to God for his wondrous love for me. I'll review my earlier journal entries that describe his character and ponder him with a grateful, humble heart.

 **Chapter 11**

We Love Others by Exhibiting Understanding

"Do not judge, or you too will be judged. For in the same way
you judge others, you will be judged, and with the measure
you use, it will be measured to you. Why do you look at the
speck of sawdust in your brother's eye and pay no attention
to the plank in your own eye? How can you say to your
brother, 'Let me take the speck out of your eye,' when all
the time there is a plank in your own eye? You hypocrite,
first take the plank out of your own eye, and then you will
see clearly to remove the speck from your brother's eye."

Matthew 7:1–5

*The first thing God does is forcibly remove any insincerity,
pride, and vanity from my life. And the Holy Spirit reveals to
me that God loved me not because I was lovable, but because
it was His nature to do so. Now He commands me to show
the same love to others by saying, "…love one another as
I have loved you." He is saying, "I will bring a number of
people around you whom you cannot respect, but you must
exhibit My love to them, just as I have exhibited it to you."*

Oswald Chambers

B eth opened up her cousin's latest social media post to catch up on how a recent family graduation party and wedding went. As she scrolled through Lacey's post, she suddenly wished she hadn't even opened it up. All sorts of thoughts ran through her mind as she looked at the photos Lacey had posted of the events. She could only hope that they would get better, but they only got worse. Some scenes from the wedding reception made her upset enough that she felt compelled to avert her eyes. *But,* Beth thought, *Lacey texted me this morning and asked me to give me her thoughts on the photos. How am I supposed to respond when these photos don't reflect the cousin I thought I knew so well?*

Shaking her head, Beth felt saddened. Why would Lacey condone this kind of behavior at her daughter's graduation and her son's wedding? What was she thinking when she posted these photos? *It feels like she's a whole different person. We were always so close and our walks with the Lord were so in sync. Help me to sort out all these feelings, Lord.*

Beth walked around her neighborhood to think and pray. *Lord, help me to not judge my cousin. Help me to understand what's changed in her life since we last met. Help me to know how to get back into her life to love and befriend her again. I don't want anyone judging me for mistakes I've made, and I don't want to cast judgment on Lacey every time I remember this post. Give me your grace, wisdom, and understanding to know how I can encourage my cousin in her faith.*

When we're confronted with a drastically different picture of someone's life with whom we thought we knew so well, it can be upsetting. Years earlier, Beth and her cousin had made their personal commitments to Christ on the same Sunday at the same church. Then they began their faith walk with Christ by doing Bible studies together, serving in their youth group, and going on summer missions projects. Perhaps most significantly, they were the only two believers in their families, which bonded them even more.

Until they grew older, got married, and moved away from each other, they had been inseparable. Beth loved Lacey and had always tried to stay in touch with her cousin and sister in the faith. Then over the years, life got busier and the miles between them reduced the times they were able to visit in person. Beth, however, assumed her cousin continued to walk faithfully with Christ. But after viewing the pictures and the immoral content depicted in them, she had to wonder.

Not knowing how to handle this situation, Beth asked the Lord for wisdom and understanding as she formulated a way to respond to Lacey. She didn't want her to feel judged—but somehow, in some way, Beth believed God would want her to talk with Lacey about what mattered most in their lives: Jesus. With a heavy heart, Beth realized she needed time to pray, and that's what she did.

The very last thing she wanted was to put up a wall between them. So she prepared for the upcoming conversation by praying every morning and every evening. She wanted to pour out her love on Lacey, but she knew that as a fellow sister in Christ, she needed to gently probe into Lacey's spiritual condition. Not because she believed she was better or holier than Lacey, but because she was afraid Lacey had abandoned her faith. *Lord, go before me in this challenging situation. Let my dear cousin know how much I love her and how much I care for her. Give me your wisdom, your understanding, so that I might help draw her back to you. Amen.*

 Take-away Action Thought

When I'm tempted to judge other believers for words and deeds that don't reflect the set-apart life that God commands, I'll ask the Lord to purify my heart motives. I will ask him to clothe me with a humble servant's heart that only desires to see my loved ones restored in fellowship with him.

A Prayer of Confession

Dear God, I'm in a difficult position. I discovered something troubling about my loved one and my heart is heavy. This isn't the same person I once knew, and I'm not sure what happened in their life to cause such changes. I'm afraid they've walked away from the faith we both shared. Help me to be wise and understanding as I prepare to talk with my loved one about these concerns. Clothe me with a humble, gentle spirit. I pray that she knows how much I love and care for her. Give me your words of life to bring her back to you. Amen.

Call to Action

Each morning and each evening this week, I'll spend time praying for the conversation I want to have with my dear one. I'll pray daily for the Lord to prepare both of our hearts and that we can be honest, teachable, and gentle with each other.

Called to Serve: We Love Others by Exhibiting Understanding

Monday: I'll pray for wisdom and understanding as to how to best approach my loved one.

Tuesday: I'll look up specific Bible passages that I can share when I talk with my dear one.

Wednesday: I'll enlist the support of several mature believers to pray along with me about this sensitive situation, without divulging any personal information that may hurt my loved one's reputation.

Thursday: I'll ask God to reveal to me if I have any known sins that I haven't yet confessed. If I do, I'll then ask for God's forgiveness.

Friday: I'll contact my dear one and ask to set up a time when we can have a long heart-to-heart chat in person if possible.

Saturday: I'll take more time to pray about what I believe God would have to say to my dear one and write down any Bible verses I might share as well.

Sunday: I'll spend this day giving thanks for this relationship. I'll then take time to remember all the good experiences we've shared and say thank-you to God for blessing me with this dear person.

 # Chapter 12

We Love Others by Showing Grace

Finally, all of you, be like-minded, be sympathetic,
love one another, be compassionate and humble. Do
not repay evil with evil or insult with insult. On the
contrary, repay evil with blessing, because to this you
were called so that you may inherit a blessing.

1 Peter 3:8–9

*Trials reveal critical things about us and wonderful things
about God. People discover that there is strength to be found
in weakness, love to be found in the midst of rejection, wisdom
to be found in the face of foolishness, and that someone
is with them even in their most profound loneliness.*

Paul David Tripp

Aimee was finishing up her paperwork for the house she
had just listed on the market—two more to go and she
would be done for the day. Her part-time real estate position allowed her to work while her four boys were in school,
and she was able to schedule the majority of her real estate ap-
pointments for the early hours of the day. She knew better than
to try and leave her rambunctious offspring alone for very long.

Lately, however, Aimee was recognizing that her sons were not only rambunctious, but that they were becoming increasingly unkind and even aggressive with one another. She shook her head in embarrassment as she recalled the earlier almost physical altercation between her oldest sons, Tyler and Trevor. It had been a peaceful morning, and they were just about to walk out the door to catch the school bus when she heard a scuffle.

Aimee knew the commotion was escalating swiftly. When she saw Tyler shove Trevor into the stovetop which was still hot from her breakfast preps before they started punching each other and their lunches went flying off the counter, she saw red. "Stop it! Stop it this instant! Tyler! Trevor! Did you hear me? Drop your bags and clean up this mess!" At the sound of their mother's voice, they reluctantly dropped their backpacks on the floor, now strewn with their demolished lunch bags. Bread, meat, cheese slices, chips, and carrots were all over the floor, along with generous smears of mustard.

While doing a poor job of cleaning up their mess, they began arguing about who got whose lunch bag. Standing over them, Aimee didn't try to hide the scowl on her face as she tersely said, "If you don't hurry, you're going to miss your bus," she said impatiently. As soon as she spoke the words, her younger sons, Timothy and Thomas, yelled that the bus had arrived.

Aimee pointed toward the door and ordered, "Go! Now!"

"But Mom," Trevor said, "we don't have any lunch."

Aimee just pointed again to the door, glaring at them.

As she watched them jump onto the bus, her heart sank. Sitting down at the kitchen table, she felt emotionally spent. After taking a few deep breaths to calm herself, she began to pray. *Lord, I get so impatient with my boys. In my heart, I know I demonstrate the same emotions toward them. Help me to learn how to handle their misbehavior without resorting to yelling and getting angry. When I react like this, I know I fall into a sinful attitude that doesn't show them what it means to love each other well. When they get home today, I need to sit them all down and ask for their forgiveness for my outburst. God give us your grace!*

Home is where character is built or destroyed. It's a hard truth, but every one of us knows that it's within our four walls that we learn from our earliest years to live out—or not live out—our faith. As every parent can attest, the behavior (or misbehavior) of our nearest and dearest can drive us to distraction and right into the path of sin if we're not careful. Aimee discovered that her reactions were her responsibility and hers alone. Yes, her four boys frequently acted out in ways dishonorable to the Lord. But when she stepped in to correct and discipline, she often fell into the same sinful, unloving responses as her children.

When we seek to serve as Jesus served—to sincerely love others and extend God's grace to them—then our thoughts, words, and deeds need to reflect that love and grace. As 1 Peter 3:8–9 says, "All of you, be like-minded, be sympathetic, love one another, be compassionate and humble. Do not repay evil with evil or insult with insult. On the contrary, repay evil with blessing." As we seek to love with grace, our thoughts toward others will shift into sympathy, and we'll respond with compassion and humility. When wronged, we'll use our God-given self-control to speak with kindness rather than anger or impatience. In short, we learn what it means to treat others as we would like to be treated. We will love our nearest and dearest more than we love ourselves.

As Aimee discovered after another heated exchange with her two older sons, she wasn't the only one who sinned. Thankfully, the conviction she felt paved the way for her to prepare her heart and mind to have a fruitful conversation with her boys that evening. She knew she had to ask for their forgiveness and then encourage them to see that their thoughts, words, and deeds needed correction as well. She wisely understood that their home is where character was being built first and best, but that only by God being present in that house would her family grow in his love and grace.

 Take-away Action Thought

When I fall into the sin of being unkind to others because I'm reacting rather than demonstrating God's grace and love, I'll confess my sin to God and immediately ask for my dear ones' forgiveness as well.

A Prayer of Confession

Dear God, please give me wisdom and divine insight to set a fresh path as to how I interact with my family. I often find myself reacting to their misbehavior in similar fashion. This is not honoring to you. I want to love my family well and learn to act rather than react, but this isn't easy for me! Please help me to have more self-control when I'm faced with emotionally charged situations. Use me as a calming, compassionate, and humble example of your love and grace. Give me your thoughts, your words, and your deeds to love them unconditionally. Amen.

Call to Action

Each morning this week, I'll begin my day by reading through 1 Peter 3:8–9 and meditating on what it means to love sincerely and in God's grace.

Called to Serve: We Love Others by Showing Grace

Monday: I'll read 1 Peter 3:8–9 and memorize these passages so that they are in the forefront of my mind throughout the week.

Tuesday: I'll talk with my family about what it means to love one another sincerely by reading 1 Peter 3:8–9 to them and thoroughly discussing each point.

Wednesday: I'll reflect on my thoughts, words, and deeds so far this week and see how well I'm using self-control when faced with difficult family situations.

Thursday: I'll specifically pray for each of my family members as I consider how different we all are and how we struggle in unique ways to love one another.

Friday: I'll write out this 1 Peter passage and place it somewhere visible as a constant reminder on what loving sincerely through God's grace looks like in real life.

Saturday: I'll reflect on our week's conversations and set up a new family meeting as needed.

Sunday: I'll thank God for his word of life that instructs us on how we should think, speak, and act to love and extend his grace to others.

 # Chapter 13

We Love Others by Speaking the Truth in Love

Speaking the truth in love, we will grow to become in
every respect the mature body of him who is the head,
that is, Christ. From him the whole body, joined and
held together by every supporting ligament, grows and
builds itself up in love, as each part does its work.

Ephesians 4:15–16

*God's grace to us is lightning. Our grace to others is
thunder. Lightning comes first; thunder responds. We show
grace to others because He first showed grace to us.*

Randy Alcorn

Molly sat in the driver's seat with the motor running, her
eyes fixed on the rearview mirror. Tapping her fingers
on the wheel, she breathed out a loud sigh. They had
just talked about this last night, and Ben promised to have Travis
back home in time for church this time. *I can't do this anymore.*
Molly prayed silently. *Help me, Lord. Give me the words to get
through to my husband about what really matters.* Holding back

tears of frustration, she tried to calm herself down so that if Ben did arrive within the next few minutes, she could hold it together long enough to get herself and the children to church.

Exhaling loudly again, Molly looked into the backseat and noticed how seven-year-old Morgan's eyes were fixed on hers. Taking a slower, quieter breath, Molly turned around and softly said, "It's okay, Morgan. I know you don't want to be late. I'll get you there on time, I promise." As she began to turn back around, she saw Ben's SUV heading down the street toward them.

She got out of the car, trying not to look angry—although Ben pulled into their driveway a bit too fast.

"I know," he began. "I'm sorry. The game went into over-time, and I couldn't take Travis out of the game because he was pitching,"

Carefully choosing her words before she spoke, Molly said as calmly as she was able, "Ben, you know we made a commitment when we got married that Sundays would be sacred. No sports. No golfing. No boating. Church comes first. What happened? We have to work through this before it becomes a bad habit for our children as well."

With that, Molly got back into her car, buckled up, and began driving to church. It was a quiet ride to church for Molly and her two children. But it was an even quieter morning for Ben after they drove off. He knew that everything she had said was true. He knew he should have gone with them too. More importantly, he understood that he was responsible for the path his family was heading down.

Speaking the truth in love is sometimes a difficult necessity as we live out our faith with our brothers and sisters in

Christ. It's not fun. It's not comfortable. It's not pleasant. But it is necessary. Absolutely. Each of us has blind spots we don't recognize within ourselves, and so we need accountability. We need to be challenged, and sometimes we need to be rebuked. We need one another to help tear down the idols of our heart that we don't even know are there.

What a blessing it is when we have faithful family members and friends who will come to us in kindness and compassion to help us see the sin we can't see. What a gift it is to have people in our lives who will help us get back on track after we've wandered away from the Lord's path. What an eternal difference it makes in our lives and theirs when we respond with humility and a repentant heart.

This principle of speaking the truth in love is just another facet of serving as Jesus served, even when it might get messy and or uncomfortable. Out of our devotion to Jesus, we prayerfully ask him to go before us. May God equip us to speak the truth lovingly, kindly, compassionately, and with abundant grace. May God prepare our hearts so that we're ready to speak, ready to listen, and ready to get back on the right path.

✿ Take-away Action Thought

When I see my brother or sister in the Lord sinning, I'll pray that God would prepare the way for me to gently speak the truth in love to this person. I will pave the way for the conversation by bathing it in prayer before I speak a single word.

A Prayer of Confession

Dear God, help me to have the wisdom and courage to speak the truth in love with my dear one. I sometimes get nervous thinking about having to have this difficult conversation. But I know that you're leading me to speak honestly because my loved one is heading down a path that's taking them farther and farther from you. Give me the right words, the right timing, and the right delivery so that this person can hear what I'm saying. Clothe me with humility, gentleness, and a sincere heart that only seeks my loved one's best. Go before me, Lord, I pray. Amen.

Call to Action

This week, I will spend time each day asking the Lord to give me his divine direction on when and how to proceed in speaking the truth in love to anyone I see heading down a destructive path. I'll prepare for my upcoming conversation in prayer so that I'm spiritually equipped to speak in love and that my loved one has ears to hear.

Called to Serve: We Love Others by Speaking the Truth in Love

Monday: I'll start this week by reading and then memorizing Ephesians 4:15–16. I want to immerse myself in this godly truth and take the time needed to truly understand how vital it is to a healthy, vibrant interchange with fellow believers in Christ.

Tuesday: I'll ask the Lord if there is anyone close to me with whom he has been urging me to speak the truth in love, but that I've been hesitating or disobeying him. I'll take time to pray through my concerns and ask for his divine grace and wisdom to know how to move forward.

Wednesday: If God has been urging me to speak the truth in love to someone close to me, I'll ask for wisdom and prayer support from a mature Christian friend before I proceed. I'll ask for their wise counsel to make sure I'm handling the situation correctly from a biblical standpoint.

Thursday: I'll ask my dear one to set a time to meet with me so that we can talk.

Friday: I'll make praying for this upcoming meeting my top priority. I'll ask for wisdom and insight. I'll ask for just the right words to speak and that my unconditional love for this person will be apparent.

Saturday: I'll focus on preparing the Scripture verses that will help my dear one see the error of their ways. I'll write them out and study them so that I'm prepared to share the truth in love in a way that demonstrates God's best for them as written in his word.

Sunday: I'll read through the book of Proverbs on wise living so that I'll be better equipped to share with others God's holy pattern for daily life and daily choices that bring blessing to our lives.

 # Chapter 14

We Love Others by Depending on God

Trust in the LORD with all your heart
and lean not on your own understanding;
in all your ways submit to him,
and he will make your paths straight.

Proverbs 3:5–6

*We must depend upon God to do for us what we cannot do
for ourselves. We must, to the same degree, depend on Him to
enable us to do what we must do for ourselves. There are times
when we can do nothing, and there are times when we must
work. In both instances we are equally dependent upon God.*

Jerry Bridges

Adam and his wife, Rachel, had just moved from Canada to the United States for a new ministry position. From their perspective, it was God's perfect timing that this position opened up in the same state in which they both grew up and immediately following Adam's graduation from seminary. Rachel was six months pregnant with their third child and was excited to be relocating so close to their families. Every day at dinner, they talked about how wonderful it was going to be for

Adam in his new job and for Rachel to be close to family and friends. From every angle, this decision to accept the managerial position for a counseling ministry felt like a gift from God.

Within six short weeks, Adam, Rachel, and their two elementary-aged children moved from a two-bedroom campus apartment into a house with a yard! Adam and Rachel started each day giving thanks to God for his timing and his blessed provision. Then, two weeks to the day of Adam's start date, everything that could go wrong did.

Will, who was set to mentor Adam for at least six months, suffered a major heart attack and was immediately forced to retire. Then, for various reasons, three of the most experienced counselors quit. As he drove home that dismal winter afternoon, he felt the bitter chill of the weather seep into his bones.

As he replayed in his mind what happened that day, he felt utterly overwhelmed by the tasks before him. He kept thinking of all the ways that he wasn't ready to lead this ministry. With three of the best counselors quitting, he had no idea how they could handle the caseloads they already had, let alone any new ones. They surely couldn't afford to take on any new counselors any time soon. *Lord, I can't do this! It's impossible.*

Suddenly, what Adam and Rachel believed had been the perfect provision from God turned into a nightmare of huge proportions. Pulling into his driveway, Adam spotted his children in the yard happily playing as Rachel sat on the front porch all bundled up and snug under a blanket. *How do I tell her, Lord? I don't want Rachel to worry, but I'm worried!*

We are servants when we depend on God. This truth can be alternately comforting and terrifying. Of course, we tell ourselves that we are totally dependent upon God. More honestly, we don't continually live with that biblical truth in the forefront of our thoughts, words, and deeds. It's the everyday tasks that are so common, taken for granted, that we tackle without much awareness that God enables us to complete even the smallest task, such as breathing. Everything. Every little and big thing is held together by the word of his power.

Yet we frequently forget that it is God who enables us to wake up each morning. It's his supernatural power, grace, and strength that equips us for whatever we set our hands to accomplish. According to the Lord's plans for us, we are truly at his mercy. We make our plans, and God decides if our plans will prevail.

The frustration comes when we, like Adam, make plans believing they are God's will for us, but then God allows these unexpected, unwanted, and often confusing detours. We find ourselves falling apart because we hadn't envisioned these trials and we feel confused, discouraged, and inadequate. The truth is that we *are* inadequate. But God isn't.

Just as Adam eventually discovered, the days and weeks that followed would surprise him. Each day, he walked into his challenging work situation having no idea how God would supply his and his colleagues' needs. But God did. Each evening, Adam would testify to God's empowerment, involvement, and constant supply of wisdom, strength, and grace that enabled Adam to serve those sought biblical counsel. Was it what Adam had dreamed about or expected when he said that yes to taking the job? No. It was better. Only after months of working and serving the community did Adam eventually say, "God's plans were different from mine, and they were better!" If we're honest about it, when God's plans prevail, we know they always are the best.

❀ Take-away Action Thought

When I feel scared and overwhelmed by the tasks before me, I'll remember Proverbs 19:31, which reminds me that although I may make plans for my life, only God's plans will prevail. This truth brings me comfort.

A Prayer of Confession

Dear God, today my plans were totally disrupted, and I felt like I was coming undone. I prayed and you answered. I walked into this situation believing that everything would go smoothly, but the opposite happened. All my well-laid plans fell apart, and now I feel totally inadequate. To be honest, I'm also a little confused. Please help me to trust you with all that's happening. I know you work all things out for my good and your glory, but right now I'm struggling to see how any of this is good—except that I know I'm totally dependent on you. Thank you for promising to meet my every need, today and through all my tomorrows. Amen.

Call to Action

Every morning and evening this week, I'll spend time reading Proverbs and meditating on what it means to be dependent on my faithful God for everything.

Called to Serve: We Love Others by Depending on God

Monday: I'll look up verses that contain the word *dependent* on them and meditate on the many different times that God's people had to depend on him and how he supplied their every need.

Tuesday: I'll ask God to reveal to me any area where I've taken for granted my dependence on him. I'll ask him to make me fully aware that my every breath comes from and is sustained by him.

Wednesday: In my journal, I'll write down all the emotions I'm experiencing right now and how overwhelmed I'm feeling. Then I'll write out a few verses that promise God's supply and help for whatever I need.

Thursday: I'll reach out to family and close friends and ask them to pray for me during this challenging season. I'll also ask them to keep me accountable when I'm tempted to doubt God and his provision for me.

Friday: I'll prayerfully compose a list of everything that feels overwhelming and pray specifically about each one.

Saturday: I'll reflect on God's faithfulness to provide for my every need and write down those moments when I realized that God helped me accomplish my work through his strength, power, and grace.

Sunday: I'll tell others about God's faithfulness to me and give thanks for what he has done in and through me to accomplish his perfect plans.

Chapter 15

We Love Others by Surrendering to God

Therefore, I urge you, brothers and sisters, in view of
God's mercy, to offer your bodies as a living sacrifice,
holy and pleasing to God—this is your true and
proper worship. Do not conform to the pattern of this
world, but be transformed by the renewing of your
mind. Then you will be able to test and approve what
God's will is—his good, pleasing and perfect will.

Romans 12:1–2

All to Jesus I surrender
All to Him I freely give
I will ever love and trust Him
In His presence daily live
I surrender all
I surrender all
All to Thee
My blessed Savior
I surrender all

Judson W. Van DeVenter

Marisa tried to keep her hands from shaking as her attorney went over the final divorce settlement details with her and Greg. Taking slow, deep breaths, she wanted to run from the room weeping. She wanted to rip to shreds the legal documents in front of her, as if that would stop this nightmare from becoming a reality. But she was resigned to the fact that nothing she said or did today would stop Greg from dissolving their twenty-eight-year marriage.

As her attorney made notes and comments to Greg's attorney, Marisa found herself drifting away from this overwhelming scene, like she was watching from another dimension. *Surely, Lord, this can't really be happening. I don't want this divorce. I never wanted it, and I'd do anything to have another chance with Greg. I feel so lost. Help me, please. Help me.*

Her attorney's words broke her trance. Everything was now in order, he said, and the papers could be signed. From Marisa's perspective, Greg seemed unfazed by the whole encounter. It was as if he didn't care—or worse still, he didn't feel any of the pain that was shattering her heart into a million pieces.

As soon as they were done, Marisa hurried from the room and headed to the nearest stairwell. Once inside, she burst into tears. Making her way down the two flights of stairs, she rushed to her car. As she closed the door behind her, she tried to control the sharp intake of breaths she knew could become a panic attack.

Trembling, Marisa began to pray. *Lord, I know I failed miserably in my marriage. I hurt Greg with my words, with my actions, and with my temper. Please forgive me for not taking my relationship with you seriously enough all these years. I see how much damage I caused, and there's a part of me that doesn't blame Greg for wanting a divorce. I wish I could go back and change everything. But I can't. All I can do now is live in complete surrender to you. Help me to learn from my mistakes. Give* me the grace and strength I need to live out my life that pleases you in every way. Amen.

Sadly, Marisa is suffering the fallout from living her life on her own terms instead of loving as Christ loved or serving as Christ served. Though she was initially shocked by her husband's decision to divorce her, it did jolt her into action. Although Marisa had always considered herself a follower of Christ, she never offered more than lip service to her faith. Her life never changed, and she never fully submitted herself to God. Marisa had been a Christian in name only.

Countless times through the years, caring friends attempted to counsel and gently challenge Marisa about the sinful choices that were slowly destroying her marriage, her relationship with her children, and the few friendships she had, but all to no avail. Marisa stubbornly clung to her perceived rights and pushed back at anyone who tried to offer her godly advice. But it wasn't until Greg actually filed for the divorce that Marisa sat up and took notice. In those early days of shock and dismay, she reached out to a godly older woman who agreed to meet with her each week. Together, they opened the Scriptures and began reading, meditating, and memorizing God's powerful life-changing truth. For the first time in her life, Marisa felt broken, but the right kind of broken. She finally acknowledged her need for a savior and asked for forgiveness of her sins. At that glorious eternal juncture, Marisa's life changed forever.

Slowly, her faith in Christ began to change her from the inside out. As a fully surrendered Christ-follower, she started to drink in the life-giving promises throughout Scripture, and she found inner peace, resilient hope, and amazing grace. The more she delved into the Bible and all its truth, the more she changed, which others began to notice. Eventually, Marisa asked for Greg's forgiveness, and he granted it. But he wasn't willing to halt the divorce proceedings.

Even though Marisa was grief-stricken at the loss of her marriage, she now works diligently every day to seek the Lord first thing in the morning, offering herself as a living sacrifice, holy and pleasing to God—which she acknowledges is true and proper worship. She searches through Scripture for specific passages that speak directly to the battle she faces and is being transformed by the renewing of her mind. Marisa has discovered that the more she invests in her relationship with Christ, the more she realizes that God has a hope and a future for her. As a woman now fully surrendered to God, Marisa has discovered the power of gospel hope that never fails.

Take-away Action Thought

When I feel overwhelmed by regret and struggle to accept God's perfect will for my life, I will read Romans 12:1–2 to remind myself that my life and all that I am belong to God.

A Prayer of Confession

Dear God, please help me to come to terms with the truth that my life and all that I am belongs to you. As my Savior and Lord, you have full rights and authority over me because I belong to you. Help me to find comfort and consolation in this biblical truth. Let me never run from my past or hide from you in shame or regret over my sins. Instead, give me minute-by-minute grace and wisdom to run to you. I have so many regrets, and I've confessed them all, but I need to let them rest in the past. Please continue to transform my mind daily and give me the wisdom and strength to walk in your path from this day forward. Amen.

Call to Action

"Complete surrender" will be the term at the forefront of my thoughts this week, and I will pray each morning for the Lord to renew my mind so that I can discern what his good, pleasing, and perfect will is for me.

Called to Serve: We Love Others by Surrendering to God

Monday: I'll start off my week by offering a prayer of confession for any resistance or reluctance I've been harboring in my heart.

Tuesday: I'll search the Scriptures for the definition of surrender to God as his child, and I'll study these passages to gain a fuller understanding of this biblical truth.

Wednesday: I'll prayerfully consider anyone from whom I need to ask forgiveness because of my stubborn unwillingness to submit to God.

Thursday: I'll memorize Romans 12:1–2 and carry these verses on a card with me throughout the day as a frequent reminder.

Friday: I'll call a wise friend and ask for accountability in both my attitude and actions and for encouragement to follow the Lord and his leading in my life.

Saturday: I'll take time to record in my journal all the good that God has brought into my life.

Sunday: I'll look up the complete lyrics to "I Surrender All" and meditate on them—and then I'll raise my voice in worship to the Lord!

 **Chapter 16**

We Love Others by Trusting in God

"But blessed is the one who trusts in the LORD,
whose confidence is in him.
They will be like a tree planted by the water
that sends out its roots by the stream.
It does not fear when heat comes;
its leaves are always green.
It has no worries in a year of drought
and never fails to bear fruit."
Jeremiah 17:7–8

*Hope is not found just in the beauty of those promises, but
in the incalculable power and authority of the One who
has made them. There is no hope in the promises of one
who has little power over the situations and locations
where they must be delivered. But you can hope because
your Lord has complete rule over all the places where
you will need his promises to become your reality.*

Paul David Tripp

J ess stood with the pitchfork in her hand and surveyed her
horses' now clean and empty stalls. "At least that's done,"
she murmured as she eyed the chicken coop as her next
cleanup chore before the afternoon storm hit. Securing the latch
tightly in preparation of the predicted high winds, she scanned
her property looking for anything that might fly away during
the storm.

Once back inside, Jess removed her boots and hung up
her weathered overcoat in the mudroom and then started making rounds through the house, checking all the windows to be
certain they were also shut fast. As soon as she was sure that
everything inside and outside was prepared for the nor'easter
heading their way, she went to the kitchen and made herself a
strong cup of coffee.

As she sipped the coffee, gazing out the window at the dark
clouds gathering from the north, she wondered if she should be
drinking any caffeine right now. She was already feeling anxious
about Todd being two hundred miles away on business, and
now this big storm was heading their way. The last time a nasty
nor'easter hit while Todd was gone, they lost electricity for several days and she had to lug their cumbersome generator from
the barn to the house—and then she couldn't get it started! What
a nightmare that had been. Jess resorted to calling her elderly
father to drive over to set it up so that she wouldn't lose all their
food in their two freezers. Just as crucially, she needed to run
extension cords to the out-buildings so the animals' drinking
water wouldn't freeze. Jess tried to push aside this rising panic
by intentionally turning her thoughts to something productive
not paralyzing.

Before Todd left for his work trip, he had taken time to
update their what-to-do-in-an-emergency list. He had written
down phone numbers of professional companies and personal
friends prepared to show up if needed. Todd had even invested

in a generator that was attached to their furnace to make it easier for her. What touched her the most was that he took time to write out in his perfect handwriting a dozen Bible verses that countered fear with faith. It was this sheet of paper that Todd had placed on their refrigerator that kept Jess's attention that stormy afternoon.

As she read the verses, her pounding heart slowed, and she experienced an unfamiliar calm. *Lord, no matter what happens or doesn't happen, I know I'm safe and secure in you. I can weather this storm and all it brings because you have promised never to leave me or forsake me. And I believe you when you promise that you will meet my every need. I will rest securely in that truth.*

We are servants of the Most High when we learn to live by faith rather than fear. We resemble our Lord Jesus Christ when we remain calm in the face of the storms of life that come our way. We reflect his faithfulness when others observe our inner peace despite the challenges, difficulties, and dangers that are part and parcel of this broken, sin-ridden world. Yes, we can live by faith even when adversaries assault us both, from within and without.

Jess learned a hard lesson during the previous storms that assailed her when Todd was away. She tried to fight down the fear that threatened her well-being even more than bad weather. Jess knew the real fight for experiencing peace and calm was an inside battle that she had to fight within her heart and mind. So she began turning toward the Lord and his word whenever those stubborn fears started to raise their ugly heads inside of her mind. She began to take God at his word as she read his promises out loud, and then as she silently meditated on them until she could repeat them whenever she started to feel afraid.

Although Jess's situation may be unique to her, we all face the storms of fear in our lives, and they come in various shapes and sizes. For some, it may be unsaved family members for whom we have prayed for many years. For others, it may be a savings account that's been depleted by job loss or unexpected financial demands we hadn't foreseen. But no matter what our particular brand of fear, we can know, really know, God's perfect peace and calm in the middle of the storm (in the middle of any crisis) because God promises to meet our every need. Be it a cloudless, sun-drenched day or a thunderous, stormy night, God promises to supply what we need—and he never lies.

✿ Take-away Action Thought

When I feel afraid, I'll immediately retreat to a quiet place to spend time reading God's word and meditate on those verses that promise me his perfect protection and provision, come what may.

A Prayer of Confession

Dear God, I have to confess that I'm feeling overcome by fear again today. I know that being alone is a challenge for me, but I had hoped that I had gotten past this anxiety. I want to trust you all the time. But admittedly, I find it hard to do. I would rather get busy preparing than accept the fact that you're in control and I'm not. Please help me to find all my safety and security in you, not in myself or in others. Please help me to find comfort in knowing that you alone are sovereign over all, and that this is a good thing. My confidence is in you alone, and I give thanks for that truth. Amen.

Call to Action

As I face my fears this week, I will be intentional about making time to be alone with God my priority each and every day so that I'm equipped to face whatever storms may come.

Called to Serve: We Love Others by Trusting in God

Monday: I'll begin this week with a prayer of confession as I prayerfully recall the many times I've given way to fear instead of leaning fully on the grace and strength that God provides for those who seek him.

Tuesday: I'll prayerfully consider the week ahead and pray about any circumstances or challenging situations before me. My utmost desire is to trust in God because he is worthy of my trust.

Wednesday: I'll spend a few moments every hour reading and rereading those verses that speak of God's perfection provision and protection.

Thursday: I'll pray for those close to me who are facing seemingly impossible situations. I'll ask God to give them his perfect peace despite the trials that surround them.

Friday: I'll contact those individuals I've prayed for this week, and I'll have specific verses ready to share with them as we talk.

Saturday: I'll reflect on my week and ask the Lord to reveal to me what I put my trust in as I walked through various challenges. I'll thank him for showing me my heart struggles, and then I'll commit to being more intentional about seeking him first when I feel afraid.

Sunday: I will rest in Jesus. I will read his word and spend time writing in my journal about the past week—how his promises gave me peace and calm despite the storms I encountered.

 # Chapter 17

We Love Others by Hoping in God

> The Spirit of the Sovereign LORD is on me,
> because the LORD has anointed me
> to proclaim good news to the poor.
> He has sent me to bind up the brokenhearted,
> to proclaim freedom for the captives
> and release from darkness for the prisoners,
> to proclaim the year of the LORD's favor.
>
> Isaiah 61:1–2

The Process of Change: Engage the battle. Separate from the object of your affections. Turn to Christ and commit yourself to keep turning to Christ. Surround yourself with wise counselors. Be part of a church. Speak honestly. Uncover the more subtle lies. Commit yourself to thinking God's thoughts about addictions and wise living. Engage the battle at the level of the imagination. Delight in the fear of the Lord.

Edward Welch

Since Becca now lived all the way across the country, she knew her mom was worried she wouldn't be able to help her. Becca also knew that she hated to see her daughter suffer, and a part of her hoped that she'd be okay on her own this time, without interference. Over the years, cycles of alcohol abuse and ever-changing jobs had landed Becca in more than one rehabilitation facility. But this time, Becca was confident things would be different. It would still be just as hard to break the old habits, but now she had a hope that didn't come from her own strength. For the first time in over fifteen years, she truly believed that things could be better.

Becca remembered Maria, a counselor who came from a nearby church to lead their evening group sessions every Thursday. With her, she brought the gospel message and a variety of homemade snacks, and a friendliness that defied the dismal circumstances of those sitting around the circle. Something about how she spoke about Jesus Christ caught Becca's attention.

Maria would open the meeting in prayer and share bits of her own story. One by one, women in the group shared their own stories—of failed marriages, abandoned children, lost opportunities, estranged families, and a persistent lack of hope for a healthy future. What amazed Becca was that despite these terrible stories, Maria found a way to point them all to hope in Christ. Becca pondered Maria's words about fresh beginnings and about the God who came to earth as a man to freely suffer and die for her sins.

During the next few weeks, Becca lost sleep as she wrestled with questions of faith and her own life. During one such sleepless night, she asked Jesus to forgive her sins and accept her as daughter and heir. Several months later, she graduated from her rehabilitation program and was hopeful about this restart in life. Becca and Maria had developed a plan for long-term sobriety. It was a multi-step, daily progress plan that included practical steps and intentional spiritual practices to keep Becca close to other mature Christian believers for accountability and encouragement. She felt wrapped in love and wanted her mom to know the same kind of eternal security through a personal relationship with Jesus. It was a new day. A new season. A new hope. Thank the Lord!

What a story of hope and redemption! And the most wonderful part of this true story is that the forgiveness and hope that Becca found in Christ is available to everyone who calls on the name of Jesus to be saved. While Becca's past was marred by repeated seasons of relapse and defeat, her faith helped her overcome what she could not do alone. Today, Becca has the empowerment of the Holy Spirit to strengthen her, encourage her, comfort her, teach her, and convict her. Never again will she be left alone to fight the battle for sobriety or against a hopeless future.

But fight she would. From her past struggles to break free from her addictions, she knew it was a daily (sometimes hourly) battle against succumbing to the temptation to find comfort and temporary peace in a bottle or a pill. Her new friend Maria was key in helping her develop a sound plan for leaving that death cycle behind. Straight from Scripture, Maria shared with Becca some essential steps she needed to incorporate into her daily life.

First and foremost, Becca had to choose to spend time with God every day, reading the Bible and praying. She needed to be in the company of other believers by attending a local church and serving there. The hardest part was being transparent about her struggles to her family and friends. But it was a brand-new life—a brand-new hope!

 Take-away Action Thought

When I begin to feel that I can't overcome my idols and addictions, I'll call a Christian friend for support and wise counsel. I'll then spend time in God's word, meditating on his glorious promises of his perfect love, provision, and power to enable me to overcome.

A Prayer of Confession

Dear God, it's me again, starting a new day! I'm so thankful that I can call you my heavenly Father and that you hear my every prayer. Never before have I had the hope I now have, and for this reason, I know that today can be different. I can nurture this hope growing within my heart and mind. I know that some days are going to be difficult. I know I will fail at times. But the greater truth is that I belong to you forever, and you have promised to never leave me. With you living in me, I am secure. I am loved. I am free. Thank you, Lord! Amen.

Call to Action

Each morning this week, I will open my Bible and read through the second chapter of Titus. I'll take my time and meditate on the truth that no matter how spotted my past is, Jesus gives me everything I need to overcome my temptations and my sins. What a glorious hope!

Called to Serve: We Love Others by Hoping in God

Monday: I'll begin my week by separating myself from the object of my desire to the best of my ability.

Tuesday: I'll turn to Christ first thing in the morning and then every hour, no matter where I am. I'll stop and offer a brief prayer for grace and strength.

Wednesday: I'll contact other Christians and share any struggles or challenges I'm facing and ask for their prayer support.

Thursday: If I've not made church attendance and involvement a priority before, I'll start today. I'll start serving alongside my fellow believers to encourage them as they seek to encourage me.

Friday: I'll ask the Lord to reveal to me any lies I may be telling myself about my addiction. I'll then share these insights with my accountability partner.

Saturday: I'll choose several Bible passages that tell of God's perfect love, provision, and power to set me free from my addiction.

Sunday: I'll spend time praising the Lord for his continuing good work within me. I'll sing praises that specifically speak of the hope I have in Jesus.

 **Chapter 18**

We Love Others by Embracing Today

"Seek first his kingdom and his righteousness, and all these
things will be given to you as well. Therefore do not worry
about tomorrow, for tomorrow will worry about itself.
Each day has enough trouble of its own."
Matthew 6:33–34

*Problem-solving is your opportunity to discern God, know
God, and mature in God while seeking to understand
what He has in store for you. And because you are working
above the net of God's grace, you can confidently move
forward knowing that all will be well with your soul.*
Rick Thomas

Jon sat frowning as he reviewed the bills laid out on the table.
There were so many expenses he hadn't foreseen when he
gave his two weeks' notice. Earlier in the year, he had accepted a position as primary accounting department head at a
finance startup. When Jon was hired to replace another em-
ployee who had suddenly quit, he later found out about an entire succession of disgruntled people who left because of failed

promises and poor working conditions. Sadly, he had no clue what a mess he was walking into on his first day.

After six months of attempting to revamp the accounting department from the bottom up, Jon realized one sleepless night (among many) that he was fooling himself into believing that he could make a real change. His boss wouldn't grant him the authority to improve the workplace, nor would he approve of Jon's suggestions that would make the department run more efficiently. At the end of the day, as he realized just how tied his hands were, Jon wondered why they even hired him!

Although Jon appealed respectfully (and from his vantage point, persuasively) to his boss, it was to no avail. After weeks of being put through the ringer, Jon handed in his resignation, believing with all his heart that God would provide another job for him. With the support of his family, close friends, and pastor, Jon felt immense relief after he walked out the door for the last time. His relief, however, was short-lived. The job-searching process and stress of unemployment weighed heavily on him. Jon never expected the transition to be easy or without some struggle. But as the days passed, he began to grow restless and started complaining to God about what he had to endure.

Every morning since high school, Jon had faithfully spent time in God's word and prayer before heading to school or a job. These days, without the scheduled routine he was so used to, he found himself struggling to maintain this lifelong spiritual discipline. He was slowly spiraling into defeat and a depressive episode, and he began second-guessing his decision to quit. Thankfully, Jon recognized what was happening and called his close friend Eric for encouragement, godly counsel, and daily reminders to be on the lookout for all the good God was still doing in his life. Eric, having been through his own season of unemployment, could readily identify with everything Jon was experiencing. So Eric gave his friend the same advice he received from others: "Start every day by giving thanks to God for every single blessing you can identify in your life. Say them out loud. Write them down. Then read and reread them. Kick the grumbling, complaining spirit out before it takes hold and takes root. Then watch and see what God will do within your heart."

God loves for his people to be thankful, no matter what they're facing. It's good for us to remember our history because it's a safeguard against sins of the past and a reflection of God's faithfulness, goodness, and grace in times of struggle. Consider the Israelites, who too soon forgot how God miraculously rescued them from the hands of the Egyptians. They grumbled, complained, and forgot it all. From our perspective, it seems shocking that these once enslaved Israelites could ever doubt God's protection after having heard the great testimonies of the generation before them. But they did forget, as do we.

Hand in hand with remembering well is being able to spot gratitude. Our God, who lives beyond the constraints of time, understands that believers in today's world face the same challenges of trusting, believing, and walking in faith as the Old Testament Israelites. Times may alter and change, but the human heart is ever the same. This is why God provides these scenarios in both the Old and New Testaments for us to read, study, and reflect on for our benefit.

If we choose to obey God's commands by heeding his words to trust him, this submissive, faith-filled submissive posture of our hearts can change everything, even when nothing in our circumstances alters. We are true servants of the Most High when we embrace today, no matter what uncertainties we may face, no matter what unknowns are on edge of our tomorrows. God is always faithful to provide for our every need. God promises to walk ahead of us, to prepare the way for us, and to show us the way. Is there any better starting place than giving thanks to God?

As Jon began implementing Eric's suggestions, he started growing a more intentional, grateful heart. Jon felt at ease, even in the midst of this stress, and his eyes were soon fixed on Jesus.

 Take-away Action Thought

When I begin to feel afraid of all the uncertainties in my life, I'll start giving thanks out loud for every single blessing I can identify in my life.

A Prayer of Confession

Dear God, my life feels out of control. I'm trying to trust you with everything that matters to me, but I feel like I'm failing. I'm working hard to remember what you have done for your people in the past. You have created a long wondrous, faith history for me that I can reflect on each day. You have never failed me. Please help me to shore up my struggling faith by giving thanks to you every day. Remind me to do this during those challenging moments when I feel all alone in what I'm facing. Your word tells me that you're always close to me and that you're preparing the way for me. I love you, Lord. I want to silence my fears, stop my complaints, and embrace today with a robust, faith-strong spirit. Amen.

Call to Action

This week, I'll begin each day by giving thanks for every blessing I can identify in my life. I'll then write down in my journal specific instances of your faithfulness to me so that I'll live in daily confidence of your perfect love and provision for me.

Called to Serve: We Love Others by Embracing Today

Monday: I'll spend the first moments of my day giving thanks for Jesus' perfect sacrifice on the cross for me, which purchased my salvation.

Tuesday: As one of God's beloved children, I'll study all the rights and privileges I have now that I belong to him for all eternity.

Wednesday: In my journal, I'll write down specific notes about God's perfect provision and protection toward me.

Thursday: I'll talk to God about any fear I'm facing and those uncertainties that threaten to undo me. I'll look up stories that describe God's intimate and personal involvement in his people's lives throughout the Old Testament.

Friday: I'll ask God to help me see the eternal lessons I'm learning while I'm in this space of waiting for the next chapter of my life to start.

Saturday: I'll embrace today fully despite any temptations I may have to grumble or complain about what I need, confident that God knows what my true needs are and that he promises to supply every one of them.

Sunday: I'll rest in God and savor this day to spend quiet moments reading the Bible, praying, and reflecting on his goodness.

✿ Chapter 19

We Love Others by Abiding in Christ

"I am the true vine, and my Father is the gardener. He cuts
off every branch in me that bears no fruit, while every branch
that does bear fruit he prunes so that it will be even more
fruitful. You are already clean because of the word I have
spoken to you. Remain in me, as I also remain in you. No
branch can bear fruit by itself; it must remain in the vine.
Neither can you bear fruit unless you remain in me."

John 15:1–4

*People had only to look at Jesus to see what God is like. People
today should only have to look at us to see what Jesus is like.
For better or worse, they'll draw conclusions about Christ
from what they see in us. If we fail the grace test, we fail to
be Christlike. If we fail the truth test, we fail to be Christlike.
If we pass both tests, we're like Jesus. A grace-starved,
truth-starved world needs Jesus, full of grace and truth.*

Randy Alcorn

Renee opened the medical app that held the latest test
results from a recent visit to her physician. She had no
desire to see her suspicions in writing, but she couldn't

go on waiting in uncertainty. *Lord*, she prayed, *you know I don't want to trust you on this, but I will.* She had been planning for three years to serve on a yearlong mission trip with her friend Jill. But now that she had prepared for the trip and raised all the money she needed, she had contracted a mystery disease. Serving on the mission field had been her dream since college, and after all her hard work, things were still out of her control. *Please, Lord, please, help me to accept whatever you choose for me.*

Renee took a deep breath and opened the app. The blood work and scans were inconclusive. Without results, she was unlikely to receive clearance to travel internationally. In her frustration, Renee called Jill and explained the situation.

Jill listened quietly and then said, "Renee, I'm so sorry your doctor still doesn't know what's going on in your body. I was hoping the tests would clear you to leave with us next month. But we both know that God knows what's going on and that we can trust him with this challenging situation. Right?"

Renee knew her friend was correct. She also knew that it was a lot easier for Jill to speak truth to her, since she wasn't the one affected. Renee prayed: *This has been my dream for so many years. You can't just remove me from the equation. Please don't, Lord. Help me to get the answers I need so that I'm able to go and serve you overseas as we planned.* After a few moments of silence, Renee finally answered Jill. "I know that you're right. It's just so discouraging to be so close to leaving and then have it snatched out from beneath me. What did we hear on Sunday? Something about learning to abide in Christ even when life doesn't make sense, and then we can demonstrate to the world what God is like when we trust him."

Jill too recalled the powerful sermon their pastor gave just a few days earlier. "Don't forget the last part when he reminded us that God is the master gardener and that Jesus is the vine.

We can't effectively serve him if we don't allow him to prune us as we prepare to serve."

Renee nodded her head in agreement. "Yes, you're right. How can I expect to be effective overseas if I can't even handle the pruning process at home? He knows the path I'd prefer, but I have to learn to abide in him."

We can only truly love others when we abide in Christ. This abiding in Jesus means surrendering all to him day by day, moment by moment. We trust him to prune us as he sees fit. This pruning is painful, though, and it often means dying to oneself (and one's dreams and desires) so that Jesus can make us all the more effective for him. As we choose to abide in him, we submit ourselves to God's perfect plan for us. Despite the fact that it may not make sense from our perspective, we can be confident that as we lay down our dreams at his feet, he'll continue the good work within us for our good and his glory.

As we submit willingly to the pruning process, Jesus, who is full of grace and truth, will shine all the more brightly in us and through us. Those around us will see that no matter what disappointments or setbacks take place in our lives, we continue to abide in him. As Randy Alcorn puts it so succinctly, "A grace-starved, truth-starved world needs Jesus, full of grace and truth." What about this God of theirs makes Christians ready and willing to surrender all to him?

❀ Take-away Action Thought

When I feel tempted to distrust God when life takes an uncertain turn, I'll remind myself that Jesus is continually pruning me for greater, more effective service. Despite my personal disappointments, I'll choose to abide in him.

A Prayer of Confession

Dear God, help me to trust you during this time of uncertainty and disappointment. I've worked so long to be able to fulfill this dream, and part of me doesn't understand why you might put an end to this desire even before I've started. But I know that you know what is best for me. You know me better than anyone, and perhaps my heart needs pruning right now. Please give me the wisdom to graciously submit to your perfect plan for me. Help me to simply be content to abide in you no matter what you've planned for me. I want to serve you, whether it's right here in my backyard or in a land far away. Let my heart reflect your grace and truth. Amen.

Call to Action

This week, I'll spend time daily pouring over God's word, specifically studying what it means to be full of grace and truth as a follower of Jesus who abides in him. I'll read stories about when God's chosen people submitted to his plan for them and how he brought about the best, even when it meant they had to relinquish their desires.

Called to Serve: We Love Others by Abiding in Christ

Monday: I'll pray for a willing and submissive heart, ready to relinquish my dreams and desires to God.

Tuesday: I'll look for verses that contain the word *abide*. I'll then copy them into my journal and then reread them as I linger in God's presence.

Wednesday: I'll study the biblical accounts of those who willingly submitted their plans, dreams, and desires in favor of God's perfect plan for them.

Thursday: I'll pray specifically for the Lord to do the pruning work in my heart as he sees fit so that I'll be a more effective servant.

Friday: I'll read John 15:1–4 and meditate on what it means to be totally dependent on Jesus as the vine.

Saturday: I'll reflect on this week and my attitude and words to others when I spoke about my problem. I'll ask the Lord to show me if I failed to reflect Jesus well by how I'm responding to this challenge.

Sunday: I'll pray that God's will be accomplished, even if that means my dreams are set aside in favor of his perfect plans for me.

 Chapter 20

We Love Others by Keeping Our Eyes Heavenward

In all these things we are more than conquerors through him who loved us. For I am convinced that neither death nor life, neither angels nor demons, neither the present nor the future, nor any powers, neither height nor depth, nor anything else in all creation, will be able to separate us from the love of God that is in Christ Jesus our Lord.

Romans 8:37–39

The biblical doctrine of Heaven is about the future, but it has tremendous benefits here and now. If we grasp it, it will shift our center of gravity and radically change our perspective on life. This is what the Bible calls "hope." Don't place your hope in favorable circumstances, which cannot and will not last. Place your hope in Christ and his promises. He will return, and we will be resurrected to life on the New Earth, where we will behold God's face and joyfully serve him forever.

Randy Alcorn

Danielle always looked forward to her mid-evening break at the factory. During that time, her grandchildren posted their answers to their online Bible study. Each Saturday, Danielle emailed to her long-distance grandchildren daily Bible readings and a question for the week. She found this ten-week study on the topic of heaven fascinating, and it helped fill out her thoughts about what the Bible says about it. She marveled at the insightful and often comical answers her grandchildren posted every day.

As she read through their posts, she realized she was learning as much about her grandchildren and how they view spiritual matters as she was about heaven. She felt it was a win-win for all of them. Danielle also loved how they tried to help one another answer the tougher questions. This had brought them so much closer together. Who knew that a Bible program like this could be not only spiritually powerful, but that it would also strengthen their family bond?

Danielle took her time to read through everything, and then she added some of her own. When one of her grandchildren misunderstood a specific Bible passage or answered a different question than asked, she gently redirected them by sharing other Bible verses or rephrased the question to make it easier to understand. Once she was finished, she spent a few minutes in silent prayer.

Thank you, Lord, for directing me to this Bible program. It was such an answer to prayer! I was so worried when my kids and grandchildren moved away that I would lose my opportunity to build into their spiritual lives. But just the opposite has happened. Since we started working through these online studies, we've grown so much closer as a family. Besides all this, I can keep up to date on how my grands think, what they believe, what they're excited about, and what they believe about you. Thank you!

When I heard this story, something inside of me jumped for joy. I considered how saddened Danielle had felt when she learned that two of her children had decided to relocate in a different state. Just like that, most of her grandchildren moved far away, and they knew that because of the distance and financial cost, they see one another only twice a year, if that. She wondered how much influence she could have on her beloved grandchildren at this distance.

So Danielle started praying. She began asking God to show her how to bridge the distance gap, and he did. Through a mutual friend, Danielle discovered a new Bible study program for all ages. She perused the site and selected several possible studies that would interest her grandchildren according to their age group. Then she emailed them individually, issuing a personal invitation for them to join her in this.

Danielle was overjoyed when all eight grandkids said yes— and an enthusiastic one at that! The very next week, they started their journey through countless Bible passages. Danielle appreciated this current study on heaven because she knew how hard the move had been on them—having to leave their home and all their friends. Through this study, she could observe how they were looking heavenward during these days of difficult transition. This pain of separation was lessening as they learned how to focus on Christ's eternal love for them.

It's never too early for us to keep our eyes heavenward, and we do well to teach our children and grandchildren about the promised new heaven and new earth. Keeping an eternal perspective helps us deal with any suffering today. When we really understand that nothing can ever separate us from the love of

God, then whatever we're going through becomes less painful. We need to remember that our eternal heavenly life is much closer than we think and more glorious than we can imagine, and that God's love will carry us along the way.

 ## Take-away Action Thought

When I begin to feel overwhelmed by the trials and suffering in this world, I'll open my Bible and read the passages that speak of the new heaven and the new earth and give thanks to God. No matter how painful this life can be, I know I'm only passing through to my permanent heavenly home.

A Prayer of Confession

Dear God, I have been feeling sad over the move my children recently made and wondering how I could continue to build into my beloved grandchildren's spiritual lives. And then you brought just the right person with just the right solution. Thank you! This was a lesson in trusting you. I'm so grateful that when I cried out to you, you made a way for me to impact my grandchildren despite the distance. Thank you for the promise of heaven and for the hope it provides me and my family. I love being up close and personal with all my grandchildren's spiritual thoughts and questions. Only you could transform what I imagined to be an unbearable change into something eternally beautiful. Amen.

Call to Action

Each evening this week, I'll spend time reading about what Jesus had to say about heaven. I'll take time to linger over these passages and let each one sink deeply into my heart and soul. I'll then give thanks that no matter what difficulty I'm enduring right now, I know it won't last forever because heaven is my eternal home.

Called to Serve: We Love Others by Keeping Our Eyes Heavenward

Monday: I'll write down anything that's challenging me or causing me to worry. Then I'll write out Romans 8:37–39 and read it in light of what I'm struggling with in life.

Tuesday: I'll look up verses that speak of heaven and write down several to carry with me through the week.

Wednesday: As I recall the verses on heaven on which I've been meditating, I'll reflect on how knowing what God has promised to his children in the future helps change my perspective on suffering in life.

Thursday: I'll share what I'm learning about keeping my eyes heavenward with a few close friends and family members who are going through their own difficulties and trials.

Friday: I'll pray for the strength and grace to endure whatever challenges and trials in which God places so that I'm a faithful, trusting reflection of Jesus to others, which will also encourage them to trust him in their trials.

Saturday: Before bedtime, I'll write in my journal any fresh insights or thoughts on how keeping my focus heavenward has helped me deal with life's struggles.

Sunday: I'll play worship music that focuses on heaven, and I'll sing along with all my heart and soul as I joyously look forward to that glorious day.

❀ Sources for Quotations

1. Paul David Tripp, *Instruments in the Redeemer's Hands* (Phillipsburg, NJ: P&R, 2002), 221–22.

2. Edward T. Welch, *A Small Book for the Anxious Heart* (Greensboro, NC: New Growth Press, 2019), 6.

3. Jerry Bridges from "Grace Quotes," https://gracequotes.org.

4. Charles Spurgeon, *Spurgeon on Prayer and Spiritual Warfare* (New Kensington: Whitaker House, 1998), 486.

5. Paul David Tripp, *New Morning Mercies: A Daily Gospel Devotional* (Wheaton: Crossway, 2014), January 26 entry.

6. John MacArthur, *Found: God's Peace* (Colorado Springs: David C. Cook, 2015), 58.

7. Randy Alcorn, *90 Days of God's Goodness: Daily Reflections That Shine on Personal Darkness* (Colorado Springs: Multnomah, 2011), 253.

8. Rick Thomas, *Change Me: The Ultimate Life-Changing Handbook* (Greer, SC: The Counseling Solutions Group, 2018), 118.

9. Tripp, *New Morning Mercies*, August 16.

10. Elisabeth Elliot, *Suffering Is Never for Nothing* (Nashville: B&H, 1989), 43.

11. Oswald Chambers, *My Utmost for His Highest* (Grand Rapids: Discovery House, 1992), May 11 entry.

12. Tripp, *Instruments in the Redeemer's Hands*, 157.

13. Randy Alcorn, *The Grace and Truth Paradox* (Sisters, OR: Multnomah, 2003), 86.

14. Jerry Bridges, *Trusting God* (Colorado Springs: NavPress, 1988), 112–13.

15. Judson W. Van DeVenter, "I Surrender All" (1896).

16. Tripp, *New Morning Mercies*, March 23 entry.

17. Edward Welch, *Addictions: A Banquet in the Grave* (Phillipsburg, NJ: P&R, 2001), 232.

18. Thomas, *Change Me*, 19.

19. Randy Alcorn, *The Grace and Truth Paradox: Responding with Christlike Balance* (Sisters, OR: Multnomah, 2003), 14.

20. Randy Alcorn, *Heaven* (Carol Stream: Tyndale House, 2004), 460–61.